EAT THAT ELEPHANT

Proven Systems for Becoming Clutter Free

VICTORIA ROSE

EAT THAT ELEPHANT

Copyright © 2014 by Victoria Rose, all rights reserved.

Victoria Rose has asserted her right under the Copyright, Designs and Patents Act 1988 to be identified as the author of this work.

No part of this book may be used or reproduced, stored in a retrieval system, or transmitted in any form or any means, electronic, mechanical, photocopying, recording, scanning, or otherwise, except as permitted by the Copyright, Designs and Patents Act 1988, without either the prior written permission of the author.

This book is sold subject to the condition that it shall not, by way of trade or otherwise, be lent, resold, hired out, or otherwise circulated without the author's prior consent in any form of binding or cover other than that in which it is published and without a similar condition, including this condition, being imposed on the subsequent purchaser.

Limit of Liability/Disclaimer of Warranty: While the author has used her best efforts in preparing this book, she makes no representations or warranties with respect to the accuracy or completeness of the contents of this book and specifically disclaim any implied warranties of merchantability or fitness for a particular purpose. Nothing within the book should be taken as advice. The suggestions and strategies contained herein may not be suitable for your situation. The author shall be liable for any loss of profit or any other commercial damages, including but not limited to special, incidental, consequential, or other damages.

Front cover elephant design by Henry Billington www.henrybillington.com.

Author's photograph by John Cassidy www.theheadshotguy.co.uk.

Author services by Pedernales Publishing, LLC www.pedernalespublishing.com

British Library Cataloguing in Publication Data.

A catalogue record for this book is available from the British Library.

Paperback edition

DEDICATION AND ACKNOWLEDGEMENTS

This book is dedicated to my two wonderful and very talented sons, Henry and Arthur Billington. They enrich my life in more ways than I could ever count. Both of them kicked me into action to undertake this project and encouraged me to share what I have learnt over many years.

They were also very keen to support me by pointing out when I was not practising what I was 'preaching'. Come on guys, we're all human and if you shoot for the stars and hit the moon, it's OK. The good news is that I got many more opportunities to use the processes I was writing about and to have even more evidence of their efficacy. I rest my case!

Many other people have supported me and I am reminded of John Donne's words:

No man is an island,
Entire of itself,
Every man is a piece of the continent,
A part of the main.

Meditation 17, 1624

To me people are always more important than things. I want to express my enormous gratitude to those who have particularly supported me to get this book to the finishing line. In alphabetical order (what else?!): Amanda Hughes, Cheryl Lanyon, Daniel Wagner and the team at 'Expert Success Towers', Ginny Barnston, Hazel Markou, Helen Turier, Humphrey Gale, John Perry, Julia Hodson, Kevin Bermingham, Liz Brown, Louise Smith, Melissa Erin Monahan, Miriam Staley, Sally Fenn, Sally Wilson and Sarah Stephens. Thank you all for your stalwart and unstinting support. At the risk of this sounding like my Oscar speech, I love you all!

I also want to thank all my clients past and present for trusting me and allowing me to walk some of the path with them. I am always delighted to hear how things keep unfolding for you all – keep in touch.

I also acknowledge my enormous debt of gratitude to Brad Brown and Roy Whitten, founders of the More to Life programme, and to all the world-class trainers I have been privileged to learn from and to serve beside. Finally to the late Susan Jeffers. I never knew her and she never knew me, but her book *Feel the Fear and Do It Anyway* literally fell at my feet in a bookshop in Tetbury more than 20 years ago and changed my life forever. It's a wonderful world.

Victoria Rose

London, March 2014

CONTENTS

Introduction *1*

1. What Clutter is and Where it Lives *7*

2. The Impact of Clutter *33*

3. Getting Started *53*

4. Tools and Techniques for Things *75*

5. Unaddressed Issues and Tasks *103*

6. The Head and the Heart Part *135*

7. Delight at the End of the Tunnel *159*

Bibliography and Resources *183*

Next Steps *185*

About the Author *187*

INTRODUCTION

In the summer of 2012 I was on holiday visiting family in Edmonton, Canada. Driving through the city one afternoon I spotted an eye-catching sign on the side of a large building: 'Reuse Centre'. I was so excited we turned the car around and went for a visit.

It was an extraordinary place. Full of everything from old sports trophies, board games, partially used reams of paper and balls of wool and carpet samples. I'd never seen anything like it. I discovered that this Reuse Centre is unique as it takes donations of unwanted items that are not accepted elsewhere. The centre has three main goals: 1) to promote the idea and benefits of reuse, 2) to provide affordable items to organisations and individuals and 3) to divert waste from landfill. As the saying goes, one man's trash is another man's treasure. Here was a facility that was enabling that transition to happen. It was truly inspirational.

My family thought it was hysterically funny that of all the wonderful things we had seen on our trip, this was one of the highlights for me. I can see why they did. Not everybody gets so enthused about seeing a huge amount of what could arguably be called clutter. But my excitement was really about the sense of possibility. There was possibility for these actual things to have a new lease of life, possibility for the people who had cleared them out to create space for something new, and possibility for the people who would find something they were missing.

Helping people move things on to create space and the possibilities this brings to their lives is my passion and my vocation. It was not surprising I was excited to witness it in action there too.

This book is about that passion but its main concern is you. My objective is to share what I have learnt in order to help you identify your clutter and to teach you ways to eliminate it. This will help you to travel a lot lighter through life and create possibilities for you to experience more fun and fulfilment and to be the man or woman who has less trash in their life and a lot more to treasure.

You may well find the process of becoming that person a challenging one. However, in this book I will share with you my unique **ROSE** system, which has helped many people over the years to declutter their lives in a shorter time than they had ever dreamed possible.

ROSE will enable you to:

RECOGNISE clutter and associated issues.

ORGANISE your things and your time.

SYSTEMISE to ensure your life flows easily and you remain clutter free.

ENJOY what you have achieved and all the possibilities now open to you.

To begin with I will explain what clutter is and where it lives. You may be aware of some of it, particularly of the physical stuff: piles of paperwork, bursting wardrobes and such like, but there are actually three categories of clutter I explore: things, tasks, and emotional clutter.

The title of this book and of my company is *Eat That Elephant* partly because the sheer amount and size of all these forms of clutter can be like having an elephant in your life that is always with you and needs a lot of looking after. It can also often be the elephant in the room that nobody is noticing – or at least not acknowledging – and the problem that it is.

The other very important reason is that the answer to the question 'How do you eat an elephant?' is also the way you will handle your clutter: a bite at a time!

You will read about the **ROSE** system as it applies to eliminating the clutter from the things you possess, the tasks you identify and from your relationships and other emotional concerns.

First I will ask you to answer 10 questions to help reveal the full impact of your 'elephant' but then I will identify the positive effects of clearing clutter and guide you step by step along the way towards them.

What you will learn is:

- How you can improve things without having to do anything. (That sounds good, doesn't it?)

- Why getting started may be the hardest part, but that by beginning with The 7 Minute Kick Start exercise you can overcome procrastination and excuses.

- My 7-Step Motivational Model to help you achieve any result you want.

- The absolute 'must have' when clearing out your life. (It's support, by the way.)

Each of the three types of clutter, things, tasks and emotional (or 'head and heart') has a chapter devoted to them and each can be read independently. However, exactly as the struggle with all clutter is ultimately inside your mind with your thoughts and emotions in charge, you will find them inter-related.

It is your thoughts and fears that will make getting started appear to be the most daunting challenge and that is why the 7-Step Motivational Model is first described in Chapter Three: Getting Started. In subsequent chapters I will go on to describe my other proven tools and techniques for organising things and then for tasks. I've also included many additional top tips along the way to keep you on track.

By following these easy steps you will not only get to the bottom of your clutter, you will see that clearing it can actually be fun and rewarding. Be warned though, it is also infectious and once you really get started and experience the satisfaction, you will want to do more!

This book is written to provide you with a helping and supportive hand at all stages of the way. We all know deep inside what we would love to do with our life and what and who we would love to have in it. Instead we often settle for what we believe we should.

Alongside over 20 years' experience of my own learning and growth in the personal development field I have supported and coached many hundreds of people. Whether we have started with the clutter inside their heads, that chatterbox that constantly comments and judges, or the physical clutter they live with, the process is always about identifying and clearing blocks.

I have distilled a lot of what I have learned into this book. I really hope you will use it for your own self-development to release your own blocks and not just for shelf-development in a dusty corner somewhere.

In the final chapter I focus on the joys and delights of living a life that is as free flowing, easy to manage and as clutter free as possible. One in which you truly get to ENJOY yourself.

So let's begin. Let's see how you can *Eat That Elephant*.

What Clutter is and Where it Lives

WHY YOU NEED TO DEFINE CLUTTER

It's a strange word 'clutter'. It doesn't exactly roll off the tongue. It's identified as coming from 15th century Middle English as a variant of clotter: 'to clot'.

We all know about blood clots having an unpleasant and undesirable effect on our health by forming a blockage, but when it comes to another source of blockage, of clotting – the 'clutter' in our everyday lives, we often fail to acknowledge it or even notice it. We fail to recognise it as the source of so much dis-satisfaction and dis-ease.

I am here to tell you that in its way undiagnosed and untreated clutter has as much of a powerful negative impact on your health and well-being as a blood clot in your body does. I don't say that lightly. It is a clot waiting to explode when it reaches a critical mass but more than that, it blocks the flow in your life, the vitality, the creativity.

In this information age our first reaction to learning of a diagnosis is often to rush to the nearest screen and click for a definition and symptoms and especially to find out what, if anything can be done about it: is it curable?

The good news in this case is yes, and we will get on to that. But to start with we really need to recognise what is clutter for **you**. What it is for me may well be different to what it is for you. So let's look at some definitions.

WHAT IT MEANS TO YOU

Dictionary definitions are always interesting and in the case of the word *clutter* offer quite judgemental words such as 'a lot of **unnecessary** or **useless** things in an **untidy** state', 'a lot of **disorganised stuff** in one place'.

But, as I said, it is what it really means to you that matters.

I might have three different wrenches in the cupboard under my sink that I never use and more than that, don't even know what they are, what they might ever be used for – or indeed how they even got there. But if you are a plumber or a mechanic they are essential tools of your trade and you might need three – or even more of them.

My idea of organisation may well be different to yours. I happen to like labelled ring binders on a shelf in matching shades – you might prefer different shapes and sizes of boxes, for instance.

It is important to state clearly here I would never presume to know what you should or shouldn't have in your possession, or how you should or shouldn't run your life. Not in this book and not if I ever work with you as a client. But what I can and will do is help you explore what is cluttering up and causing clots in your life. And then help you deal with it – a bite at a time.

HOW I SEE IT

Having talked of flow and blockages, let's start to get very specific. Using the experience I have gained working with many people over the years, I find it very useful to categorise clutter. I will explain what these categories are and then give you my own definition.

WHAT IS CLUTTER? (ENTER THE ELEPHANT)

All your 'stuff', all your unsorted things, unaddressed tasks, things on your lists (if you make them) and even the lists themselves, are cluttering up your home, your work place, your desk, your car, your computer, and especially your mind. Objects, items and issues that we seem to have little trouble accumulating but a lot of trouble dealing with.

The sheer amount and size of this clutter is like having an elephant in your life that is always with you and needs a lot of looking after. Hold that image in your head. It's very powerful (and it's why I call my company Eat That Elephant). Also it is often used to illustrate a thought process: you might have heard people say 'if you tell somebody not to think of an elephant, they always think of an elephant.'

We can all see there are many places that clutter exists around us. But what you may not be able to see is that even if you are trying to ignore it, at some level that elephant is always in your head. This is the most significant and potentially the most damaging place of all.

**My definition of clutter:
Clutter is postponed decisions**

Think about this for a moment.

By recognising some or all of the things you might class as clutter in your life you will realise that they are there because you haven't yet decided what to do about them.

It is **so** important to recognise that the first, and the most important, place clutter exists is in your head. And most of us could certainly do with a lot more space in there.

THE 3 CATEGORIES OF CLUTTER

Let's get this elephant out of our heads and begin to define a picture of it. We can see that a real elephant has ears, legs, a trunk, a tail and so on. Now we want to see what our metaphorical elephant looks like, what it feels like and where its home is. But we want to look at all its component parts separately because it can be very overwhelming when we just see the whole thing.

1. THINGS

To help us determine what things are clutter it is hard to find a more useful measure than this instruction:

'Have nothing in your house that you do not know to be useful, or believe to be beautiful.'

This is a well-known quote by William Morris, the English 19th century artist and textile designer. I find it a wonderful rule of thumb for myself and for all my clients.

With that in mind, let's list some.

- Anything you don't love, e.g. items bought in a sale primarily because they were bargains, clothes you know don't suit you, pictures on display but which no longer reflect your taste.

- Anything you don't have a use for e.g. a coffee machine and you don't drink coffee, knitting needles and wool and you don't knit, tools you can't use, gadgets.

- Anything untidy or dis-organised e.g. your desk, your underwear drawer, a storage area.

- Too much of anything in too small a space e.g. books, papers and brochures crammed onto shelves, utensils in a kitchen drawer.

- Things kept 'just in case' e.g. old clothes,

shoes, wrapping paper, bubble wrap and padded envelopes, bags, boxes, carpet offcuts, your children's old toys.

- Out of control collections e.g. anything that's there just because it has a cat/dog/elephant/sheep or whatever motif, cheap souvenirs from holidays, so much of anything that you can't catalogue or display it.

- Unwanted inheritances or gifts e.g. especially large or old fashioned pieces not in-keeping with your taste and life style, joke or novelty items.

- Accumulating piles e.g. papers and magazines, mail, clothes not put away.

- Partially used and old/out of date things e.g. cosmetics, toiletries, paints, old calendars, medicines.

- Anything broken or with missing pieces e.g. jewellery, board games, odd socks.

- Things stored by other people/commercial companies for you e.g. left behind at your parents' house, crated up when you moved.

As you read that list you may well find specific items in your own life pop into your head.

How about that pile of clothes, shoes, bags, and umbrellas you have to step over every time you come home or go out? Or the ornament that is broken but that you haven't got the special glue – or the inclination – to fix it. Then there's the skirt or trousers with a drooping hem, or a stain; the unopened mail (electronic as well as snail mail), the things on a chair you have to move in order for somebody else to sit down; an old fashioned clock that doesn't work and you don't like the look of – but it came from Granny; your children's nursery school art work drooping from the fridge when they're now at university...

You get the picture. But what you might not realise is that every single one of those things is also represented in your head and is taking up space and energy there in exactly the same way as it is in your home or workplace.

2. UNADDRESSED ISSUES AND TASKS

These can be harder to spot than objects and indeed the objects may be part and parcel, so here is a list of some things that fall into this category.

- Projects started and not finished, e.g. redesigning the garden, putting photos in an album, arranging a filing system.

- Things you want to do but haven't got round to, e.g. making a will, writing a letter, getting a policy to cover your interest-only mortgage.

- Things you need to do but haven't yet, e.g. get a handle on your financial situation.

- Things you have resolved to do but haven't done anything about, e.g. lose weight, get divorced (or married!).

- Anything you know you 'should' be doing but are avoiding, e.g. cleaning the mould off the shower tiles, filling in your tax return.

- Other people's clutter (pretty much self-explanatory!).

- Anything on your To Do list that isn't an actual next action step.

- People you spend time with but REALLY don't enjoy being with, even if you used to. Yes, people can be clutter in your life too.

3. MENTAL AND EMOTIONAL ISSUES

You might be surprised at the final category I put clutter into. But you might find it easier to recognise because it may well be causing you stress and discomfort and taking up a lot of head or heart space. Examples of these types of things are:

- Unresolved emotional issues, e.g. following up from a row you had with somebody or the ending of a relationship.

- Worrying, e.g. about anything from who to invite to a party you are having to preparing for an important presentation at work.

- Self-critical and judgemental thoughts towards yourself or others, e.g. I'm so stupid, I always say the wrong thing, she's a loud-mouth who only cares about herself.

- The little voice that chatters away inside your head – usually negatively e.g saying how tired you look, how you really shouldn't be eating that biscuit as you are fat enough already, how you really should get a better job.

- Something you are upset about and not addressing e.g. somebody said something you took as undeserved criticism and you are nursing the hurt rather than talking to them about it.

- Something you repeatedly get upset about and are not addressing e.g. you do more household tasks than your partner, the neighbours' dog regularly does a poo outside your house and they don't pick it up.

- Moaning and complaining e.g. about the weather, your partner.

- Old belief systems e.g. my father left my mother so all men are unreliable, I didn't go to university so I'm not very clever, there'll never be a black president in the Whitehouse.

- Fear e.g. of imagined outcomes, of doing something new, of failing.

- Preoccupation with trying to impress others e.g. wearing clothes you don't like but think they might, voicing opinions that aren't yours.

- Focusing your thoughts and attention on the past e.g. seeing it as the good old days when you were young and happy, or conversely dwelling on regrets and missed opportunities.

- Holding on to resentment and ill-will e.g. reliving a wrong somebody once did you, refusing to forgive.

A lot of things in these last two categories could be described as 'incompletes'.

You will know the feelings you get when something is 'incomplete': the low level constant niggle, a shifting sense in your body that's not settled or relaxed, a lot of sighing and groaning and the 'I really must' type of self-talk.

It's a very different feeling in your body when something is 'complete'. Think of a small example – that sense of satisfaction when you seal a letter, put a stamp on it and drop it in the post box; when you shut the door on the house you are moving from and everything is loaded on the removal van; when you shake hands or 'kiss and make up' because a difficulty has been resolved between you and somebody else. You know it when you have it. It is a kind of settled, satisfied sigh, a relaxed kind of feeling and it's a time to praise yourself and to enjoy ticking it off the list.

HOW TO IDENTIFY YOUR CLUTTER

As so often in life, it is easier to see things that we perceive to be an issue in other people's lives. This can help us to avoid looking at our own. But the purpose of this book is to motivate and help you to identify any clutter in your life, to identify the impact it is having and to give you some strategies to deal with it. So let's get personal.

1. YOUR THINGS

A baby first step:
When I run workshops I often begin by asking the people there to empty out their handbags, wallets or pockets. Whatever they have left the house with and are carrying around with them, often all day every day.

This is a particular issue for women and you will often hear them say 'the bigger my handbag, the more I fill it'. So as the several lipsticks, many pens, books, kindles, phones, often huge bunches of keys, bulging purses full of vouchers, receipts, entire make up kits, spare tights and so on emerge to cries of 'I wondered where that had gone,' and 'goodness, I seem to have 7 pens in here,', people begin to recognise the amount of 'stuff' they are carrying around that they really don't need with them every day. They start to recognise that this might have a part to play in their back ache or stiff neck or why their clothes don't sit as nicely as they did in the shop when the pockets were sewn up so nothing could be stuffed in there.

This is becoming more of an issue for men too now – the black backpack has taken over!

Explore Your Daily Burden

I strongly encourage you to look in whatever bag or container you regularly leave the house with and see if it really meets your actual needs and to ask what you are carrying unnecessarily.

This is a great place to start identifying – and clearing – what may be clutter in your life. So take a minute to put away the sales vouchers, throw away the used tissues, then empty and up-end the bag or wallet and shake out the muck at the bottom. Only then put the things back that you know you want and need to carry with you.

You will feel satisfied and hopefully have taken the first step on the way to travelling lighter in your life.

A bigger second step:

The next thing I invite people to do is to take a tour of

one of the places they spend most of their time in. This would typically be their home or workplace. As you are reading this and not in a workshop you may even be in one of these places right now so that will make it even easier.

If you are not actually physically there you can take a virtual tour in your imagination, your mind's eye. In order to do this first read these instructions through a few times so you become familiar with them. Then, before starting the process, close your eyes and take a few deep breaths.

Note: doing it this way may feel a little hard to do or strange at first and it can take a while to get used to. Be patient and allow yourself to settle into the process. Trust yourself and your own memory. You may be amazed at the clarity of what comes into your mind and you 'see' even when the things are not physically in front of us. We are somehow connected to all of them.

Space Exploration

1. Whether you are physically doing it or using your imagination, go to the front door – or the door you usually enter the space through. Starting here make a tour of all the rooms very slowly and taking much time. Make sure to take lots of slow deep breaths while you do this.

2. Take a good long objective and dispassionate look around. Try to distance yourself from everything you see as if you are observing it for the very first time.

3. Notice how you feel as you look around and see things with these fresh eyes. Consider what impact what you are seeing has on your life: on your time, your well-being, your frustration levels, your relationships and so on.

4. Ask yourself and make mental notes about what you would like to change, what you would like to see and how you would like to feel in this space.

5. Think how it would be if a fairy came and magically made it just like you want?

6. Consider what you would do with the time, the space, the money you have saved? What would the quality of your life be like, every day?

7. Make sure you visit every room and that you scan it carefully before moving on to the next.

8. Stop when you find yourself back at the front door again.

The third step:
It's important to recognise what you have seen. When you have finished your tour (actual or imaginary) take a few moments to note down any things that you would now define as clutter. Remember the definitions we looked at earlier.

By tuning into the physical feelings you have experienced doing this you are beginning to recognise the effect that clutter is having on you. You might notice a sinking heart, a grimace or a shrug of your shoulders. This is the key way to identify your clutter. For even if your head is saying, 'that's ok, that's not clutter', your body really knows if it is.

Even if you find you don't have many items on your list it is a very good idea to repeat the exercise of passing through the whole space. The more you look at it and recognise it for what it is, you will find clutter seems to become more 'in your face', almost brighter (even if it's covered in dust!) and harder to ignore. You will also experience more pleasure and uplift from looking at or holding the things you realise you really do love.

2. YOUR UNADDRESSED ISSUES AND TASKS

While you were doing this exercise, you may well have identified some of your own outstanding issues and tasks at the same time. Seeing an object can often trigger the recognition, for example an unopened letter from the bank may be a symbol you are not taking responsibility for your finances; the untouched brushes and pots of paint in the garage may indicate your enthusiasm for decorating the bedroom has waned. You may also see lots of pieces of paper with random notes or To Do lists on.

Now having said that To Do lists can be clutter, it may seem contrary to recommend you start another list. However, this will be a different list and is an essential part of the process. We have to recognise and capture all the issues in one place. So start with a new notepad or at the very least a clean sheet of paper (real or on your computer – though having an actual piece of paper in front of you can add any extra dimension).

Now make a list, or draw a mind map diagram if you prefer, of all the unaddressed issues and unfinished tasks that are in your head – keep on until no more come. It will be like popping corn – at first there is nothing, then a mass of kernels popping at the same time, then a gradual slow down. Then it's done.

After each item on the list it can be very helpful to keep prompting yourself with the question 'and what else?' Make the note – 'and what else?' until the popping stops. Keep the list – (and something to write with) - handy as things may well keep coming to you over time.

This is what is known as a brain dump.

3. MENTAL AND EMOTIONAL ISSUES

While objects may alert us to the recognition of tasks unfinished, it can be hardest of all to break down and identify mental and emotional clutter. It may also be alien to you to even think of it as such. But all these things are indeed clots, creating blocks of energy and blocked emotions that will most definitely be having a negative impact on your well-being.

This is my recommended way to get the mental and emotional issues identified and on to the list. While you do this, try to remain detached and regard the questions themselves and the answers that come with curiosity to avoid getting hooked into any pain or frustration or into the story around them. Be reassured that recognising and naming the issues is the vital first step on the way to resolving them.

Reflect and Recognise

- Imagine you are about to have a long conversation with your best friend. Somebody who doesn't judge you, won't interrupt or try to 'fix' you and who really cares about your happiness and your well-being. Your notepad is, for now, going to be this best friend.

- At the top of the page write the questions such a friend would ask:

- How are you feeling?

- What's been worrying you lately?

- Is there anything upsetting you?

- Is there anybody upsetting you?

- Anything dragging you down?

- If you're not feeling on top of the world, why not?

These are also the kind of questions a counsellor or therapist might ask. But here we are not heading for analysis or anything like that, we are just beginning to identify what's bothering you and what is in the way of your happiness and enjoyment. (Note of course there is the possibility you might identify an area of such concern you do need to consult a professional. You can find some useful resources at the back of the book.)

The main thing to watch out for is not to tell the story. We are so used to making a drama out of things, and fill our conversations with expressions such as 'he said', 'she said', 'then he made me…' That kind of thing – do you recognise that? But what we are after here is just the headline. So that would be something like the row with Mum, the economic situation, feelings about getting older, a son without a job, unintentionally upsetting a good friend and so on.

I hope you are fortunate enough to have at least one person in your life you feel able to talk to like this because then you will have experienced the relief of simply expressing all this stuff – and getting it out of you and into the daylight.

But it is also common for us not to do that. Many things hold us back but fear of being judged and abandoned come pretty high on the list. So the good news is nobody is here to judge you as long as you make the commitment to yourself that you won't hold back. That is why we need to try very hard to stand back and keep a distance and observe our lives from the outside with curiosity and compassion, not criticism and judgement.

So set aside some time with your notepad. Sit quietly where you will not be interrupted. And have that conversation. See what comes. And don't judge it. For each thing just say, 'wow, that's interesting. So **that's** what's bothering me'. Then 'so what else is bothering me?' And so on. As with the popcorn analogy, keep right on until the popping stops.

FUTURE POSSIBILITIES

So what next?
Now we have found out what clutter is and where it is, what can we do about it?

When potential clients approach me it is usually because they recognise that they have a problem with some kind of clutter and they don't know what to do about it.

We take time to discuss what they are experiencing and what they want and then explore the options.

The first option of course is to do absolutely nothing at

all. And that is what some decide. They just make one decision: the decision to postpone the decision!

That aside there are three more productive options I discuss with my clients:

1. They can sort things on their own.

2. They can do it together with some good support – a friend (tips on choosing one come later) or with a professional such as myself.

3. They can get somebody else to do it for them – that could also be a friend or a professional.

A big part of my purpose in writing this book is to give you some strong support and guidance through the process of decluttering. The key part of this is to provide you with a simple, proven approach.

So to help you become clutter free and achieve space, organisation and harmony in your life, as I promise on the cover of this book, I will be teaching you my own simple and proven approach which I call

Victoria's ROSE system.
ROSE stands for **R**ecognise, **O**rganise, **S**ystemise and **E**njoy!

In this chapter we have been focusing on the first step and RECOGNISING what clutter is and where it lives. You have also had a taste of what it might be like to get it under control – to eat that elephant – and live without it. We are doing it together.

I will be exploring other ways of doing it together later in this book. In particular I will examine the function – and in fact the necessity – of some kind of support for you (in addition to this book).

If you have done the exercises I suggested you will also have RECOGNISED areas you want to address and have three lists, one from each category of clutter:

- Things

- Unaddressed issues and tasks

- Mental and emotional issues

Having done all this you might already have enough motivation to get started and be keen to read on and learn about the next step. On the other hand you might have found you are harbouring a super-sized elephant of a project which will require super-sized elephant motivation and this may seem rather daunting right now. You may also have recognised there is a requirement to allocate resources to handling it. Resources of time, money and energy.

In order to get really motivated it is vital to recognise and understand the full nature of the impact that NOT addressing your clutter issues has and will have on your life and your health. In the next chapter we look at this in detail.

So if you have read this far and you are still not convinced that clutter is potentially a life-threatening issue that needs addressing, please read on.

But just before leaving Chapter One, let's summarise the main points so far:

KEY LEARNING POINTS

- Clutter in your life threatens the quality of your life and your health like a blood clot in your body does.

- What is clutter to you may not be clutter to me.

- The definition: clutter is postponed decisions.

- The three categories of clutter:

1. Things

2. Unaddressed issues and tasks

3. Mental and emotional issues

🐘 RECOGNISING and identifying your clutter is essential.

🐘 Making a list is very helpful.

🐘 There are three options to getting it done: do it yourself, do it with somebody or have it done for you.

🐘 The **ROSE** system: **R**ecognise, **O**rganise, **S**ystemise, **E**njoy!

The Impact of Clutter

WHY DOES CLUTTER AFFECT US SO PROFOUNDLY?

In Chapter One I said that having clutter in your life can have a negative impact on your health and well-being. This is similar to having a blood clot in your body.

This may seem over-dramatic to you and indeed presents quite a graphic image. I'll explain why I use it.

A clot also represents an object of fear – a silent potential killer, a rogue enemy lurking quietly. Sometimes we are conscious of places it might attack us and we take what we hope are preventative measures. For instance, we may be setting off on a long-haul flight to a longed for exotic holiday. We put a lot of focus on our special holiday and plan carefully. So we wear our in-flight anti-DVT socks, we remember to get out of our cramped seats and do some stretching, we drink lots of water to avoid dehydration, and we hope those altitude-induced clots won't happen to us. And hopefully they won't.

We are educated about the possible effects of taking a long flight, and other potential clot-causing activities. But we are rarely educated about the effects of the clutter in our lives. Sometimes in our lives we take calculated risks, such as preparing for flying. Other times we may adopt a don't care attitude about our health and think other things are more important.

But eventually a wakeup call comes. It might be quite small: we can see if we are carrying a few extra pounds when we look in the mirror, or put on an old garment and find it has suddenly become too tight; a routine medical check-up reveals our cholesterol is on the high side. But sometimes the wakeup call is BIG – and there's no ignoring it then – a stroke, or a heart attack.

The reason clutter affects us so profoundly is that we don't recognise it as the threat that it actually is. There is no publicity campaign and no medical health warnings about it.

However, although you may not be consciously aware of it, something in you does know if you've got this kind of clot. But if you are not consciously aware of it and of the cost to you, you will stay with the familiar status quo of a cluttered and disorganised life.

This chapter aims to show you the many varied and often insidious ways that living with clutter impacts you. This is a vital part of getting the motivation and determination to deal with it.

And the very good news is that the symptoms from what we think are separate issues, such as stress, can often be cured by addressing our clutter.

WHAT ARE THE EFFECTS OF CLUTTER?

Remembering that there are three categories of clutter:

- **Things**
- **Unaddressed issues and tasks**
- **Mental and emotional is**sues

The biggest negative impacts of clutter

- Physical hazards: things that are in the way. You trip over them or have to move them and they gather dust – or worse.

- A disorganised and consequently stressful life style.

- Procrastination: you may frequently feel overwhelmed and frustrated.

- Distraction: your attention is drawn to stuff and sources of anxiety. You focus on the past rather than enjoying the present and creating a bright future.

- The financial cost: buying unnecessary replacements, paying to get things cleaned, stored, insured that you don't really need.

- The time cost: wasted time looking for things, time spent looking after things – moving them around, deciding what to do with them, worrying about them.

- The health cost: you may experience feelings of tension, fatigue, lethargy, frustration, shame, anxiety, depression and feel generally weighed down, burdened and lacking in energy. You may well even carry excess weight.

- The cost to your relationships: our clutter not only has a negative impact on ourselves but on those we live and work with. It is often a cause of disagreement and dispute.

- The cost to your self-expression: how you see yourself and how you are seen by others. We spend a lot of time explaining, justifying and excusing our behaviour, and being self-critical.

- The legacy. If you don't handle these things while you are here and able to, somebody else is going to have to when you are not. Is that really what you want to gift your children, family or friends?

What effect is your clutter having on you?

I hope by reading this list you can now recognise that clutter is not just about that murky corner of the kitchen you haven't cleaned out, or the garage that needs tidying. It has many aspects and they all affect the whole of your life.

Everything around you is reflected inside your head and your body, and everything inside your head is reflected outside in your physical environment.

Understanding the full impact of this in your life is fundamental to propel you to change. There are many reasons people stay in the rut of familiarity and habit. We are comfortable with what we know but we fail to recognise that the rut is also muddy, dirty, easily waterlogged– and generally very unpleasant. Once you see what rut you are sitting in, you will want to change things fast.

So let's look at how to do this: how to move from general points to specifics about you. In real time. Let's try to identify what muddy rut you may be sitting in.

As we do so, I want you to remember that the quality of your life matters. I want to help you to live the best life you possibly can. Remember that the things in your life matter. I want you to have things you love and that enhance your life every day. Remember that the people in your life matter. I want you to have the best possible relationships.

In order to see what might be getting in the way and cluttering up your path, here are 10 questions to ask yourself:

10 questions to help reveal the full impact on you

It will really help to go back to the lists and notes you made from doing the exercises in Chapter One before you answer the following questions. And be very specific about things, people and places to really shine the light on your life.

Take your time. Write down your answers. And be VERY truthful.

1. How do you feel when you survey the state of your surroundings – light, happy, energised? Or tired and lethargic, maybe even ashamed, depressed, weighed down and burdened?

2. What specific occasions can you identify when you waste time and get frustrated looking for things you can't find, or worrying that you've forgotten something?

3. How much do you focus on the past and things associated with it rather than on enjoying the present or looking forward to the future?

4. When you know there are things to sort out, tasks to start or finish or issues that need addressing, what do you find yourself doing instead?

5. What might people say about you and how they judge the way you live if they were to be brutally honest? As an energised, fun go-getter living in a cool place, or as a bit of a slob who lives in a bit of a tip? Somebody you can trust to be straight with you or somebody who is best avoided?

6. What have you been putting off doing for a long time and why? Would you honestly say these are real reasons or merely excuses?

7. Do you have trouble packing to go away?

8. How much time, money and effort has to go in to looking after your stuff (that's cleaning it, moving it, storing it, insuring it…) and would you say the things in your life are serving you, or are you serving them?

9. What might be the impact of all of this on your physical, mental and emotional health?

10. What might be the impact on your personal and professional relationships?

Having answered all these questions, I need to counsel caution. Do not allow yourself to fall into despair or self-recrimination about the state of things.

Let's just see it as the elephant has entered the room and you are becoming aware of the full impact of that. You are just getting a clearer picture of your elephant.

The good news is that recognising your elephant will enable you to understand what it is costing you to keep it fed and watered, so to speak. Only then will you come to see that you no longer want to give it house or head space. This elephant is not an object of curiosity in the zoo or a rare creature spotted on safari but a metaphor for the brooding, over-shadowing presence of clutter in your life.

I'm going to tell you about a client of mine. Let's call her Sarah.

Sarah's 'Elephant'

Sarah lives in what would be a lovely Edwardian semi-detached house in a very pleasant residential area. She shared this with her partner until he moved out when the relationship came to an end, about a year before she contacted me.

She had never really claimed the house as her own living space since his departure. His old shaving things were still in the bathroom and items of his clothing were lurking at the bottom of her linen basket. His abandoned running machine took up a huge amount of floor space in the lounge. He had been the cook in the household and many boxes, packets, saucepans and general cooking paraphernalia were spilling over the entire kitchen. Only a tiny area of the work surface was available for use.

Sarah had had people round at Christmas. Part of her preparation for this had involved cramming huge amounts of everything into every cupboard and out of sight space, especially under the stairs. Eight months later it was all still there.

She was too embarrassed to have anybody round to her home. She travelled a lot for business and as there was nowhere to pack and unpack there were piles of clothes and work materials everywhere. She was always buying supplies at airports – beauty and hair products, tights, mobile phone chargers, travel adaptors, because she couldn't find anything.

There were also boxes and boxes of things which had belonged to her parents, who were both dead, all mixed in with day to day rubbish, dry cleaning wrappers and hangers, old mobile phones, receipts, in-flight gift bags and so forth.

Despite a bright jovial countenance she was always running to catch up with herself. She was tense, fidgety and fraught, and spent a lot of time explaining and saying how terrible it all was. She was hoping to start a new business venture and was looking for a new relationship but she was ashamed of the chaos around her. She was paralysed with indecision about what to do with any of it so spent most of her time running around and being away from home giving her time and attention to anything rather than to what was under her nose.

I want to emphasise that Sarah is an extremely nice, kind, interesting and creative woman. There is nothing at all 'wrong' with her. She had just created an elephant and allowed it to take over her home. And it wasn't a pretty sight.

So given that Sarah is a successful, charismatic woman with lots of friends, a nice enough home where she had just about enough space to get by, and a very full and busy life, why would she want to change anything?

Well just as you have done by answering the questions above, Sarah had recognised she had an elephant of a problem. She had realised the full extent of the discomfort and pain that living like this was causing her. And she'd had enough.

But moving AWAY from pain is only one motivating factor for us human beings and it can seem quite a slog sometimes. It can also be hard to maintain motivation once the initial most intense pain is relieved. But moving TOWARDS pleasure, however, that's another thing. And Sarah was keenly aware there were many pleasurable things and opportunities she wanted to enjoy in her life that she somehow just wasn't managing to create.

The combination of wanting to move away from the frustration and stress of the way she had been living and towards the life she knew she wanted had led Sarah to reach out to me for help.

The positive impact of clearing clutter

One of the first things we did together was to encourage Sarah to reflect more on the pleasure and the benefits to her of living a clutter-free life. We really got down to the depth of her desires to find a new relationship and to create her new business, working from an office in an organised beautiful home with an inviting space for people to visit.

She knew what she wanted to change and improve in her life and why.

So I invite you to do the same thing. By doing the exercise above you will have identified things you want less of. Now I recommend you take a few minutes here to set aside this book and reflect on what pleasures and positive experiences you want more of.

Remember, Sarah wanted clarity of mental and physical space to start her new business, a new relationship and for her home to look the best it could.

What do you want and why?

Write down at least three things you want to create and why you want them.

By clearing the clutter in your life you will move out of your muddy rut and have the time, space and energy to create these things.

THE BONUS BENEFITS OF CLEARING CLUTTER

Also, in the same way that shops offer reward card schemes that give you extra points every time you shop, there are extra benefits you will gain. You may be surprised, but I can assure you that as you clear your clutter – as you start to eat that elephant – you will experience the positive impact of some if not all of these benefits.

You will:
- Remove sources of regular discomfort and frustration.

- Have more time and money and use both more consciously and wisely.

- Experience improved relationships by removing areas of dispute and disagreement.

- Discover parts of you, especially the fun and creative parts, which have been buried under your 'stuff'.

- See new choices and possibilities emerge that you hadn't even thought of before.

- Feel guilt-free not guilty about things you haven't handled.

- Free a lot of stuck energy.

- Handle mundane tasks simply and easily.

- Have better health.

- Gain an improved perspective on your life – who and what REALLY matters to you.

- Find making decisions much easier.

- Enjoy yourself, your things and your life more!

After doing this exercise and focusing on the pleasures of the new ways of living that you want to create, you might hear a little doubting voice inside your mind. It may be saying things such as, 'that's too far-fetched, it's not possible and quite frankly there's just too much to do'. And indeed we do need a reality check. The pain you are experiencing with the situation at the moment is real, but the pleasures you yearn for might seem unachievable and unrealistic.

However, by taking account of reality I can assure you that you will attain the pleasure. It **is** going to take time and effort, and possibly money, to declutter, organise and systemise your life. There is no magic wand or Mary Poppins character coming to click her fingers to make it all happen in the twinkling of an eye. But there are strategies and support systems you can employ to help you get there. This book is one of them.

The reality is that it does call for you to show up and take responsibility for change in your life and actions to achieve it. If you are feeling overwhelmed or believing that it is impossible to make changes, you might find it useful to know that you can:

Improve things without having to do anything

Three simple stages.

1. Take a stand to see things just as they are. Not worse by making them a dramatic story to tell and not better by playing them down.

2. See the situation as one that is already improving and always think and speak of it like that.

3. Recognise you do not HAVE to do anything at all. But that you are making the CHOICE to create what you really want.

Just by doing this and shifting your attitude and perspective you will find the elephant isn't as huge and all enveloping as you at first thought and you can see that you are actually in charge of it. That is a big improvement. Then, strangely and miraculously, you will start to take actions that will precipitate the change you want. And you haven't **had** to do anything.

It is unlikely, but if after reading this far and doing the exercises you can honestly say to yourself that you don't want to change even a part of the clutter in your life, it is important to recognise that is a valid choice too. However, I would encourage you to question if that choice really does come from the part of you that wants only the best for you.

SO WHAT'S NEXT?

I hope by now you are eager to get started and that's exactly what the next chapter is about. Just before we do so, there is one final point I want to make about strengthening your determination.

This is about committing whole-heartedly to the process.

I recommend you find somebody to talk to about your progress so far. Be sure to tell them exactly what your choices are about: making positive impactful changes by decluttering your life.

Tell them what it means to you to address these issues. And tell them you are committing to do whatever it takes.

By making a commitment to yourself to do this you are taking a vital step onto the path. By voicing that commitment out loud to another, you make your stand even stronger. By asking somebody to bear witness to your intention and asking them to hold you accountable you are much more likely to succeed.

This is a fundamental principle of support and a function I provide to all my clients. It is even more powerful to do this with somebody who is emotionally detached from you and can therefore be more neutral and provide tougher support as and when required. I strongly recommend you can find somebody to provide this for you.

KEY LEARNING POINTS

- 🐘 Clutter affects us profoundly because we do not recognise it for the threat it poses.

- It has negative effects on your whole life.

- Clutter inside your head is reflected in your outer environment, and clutter in your environment leads to a cluttered mind.

- Understanding the full impact on your life is fundamental to initiating change.

- Moving away from pain and towards pleasure are both motivators.

- There are many positive impacts and benefits of clearing your clutter.

- You have to take responsibility for change and action.

- You can improve things just by changing your attitude and your language.

- Making a commitment to yourself and to another is a great foundation to begin making positive impactful changes.

Now let's get started!

Getting Started

WHY GETTING STARTED CAN BE THE HARDEST PART

It's a funny thing, but I found getting started to write this chapter actually really hard. How ironic! Here am I writing about getting started and I have been doing pretty much anything but.

People say JFDI (Just F***ing Do It!), make it a priority and go for it, you can do it, just start writing and it will flow, you've talked about it, now make the time and get on with it. Comments like these, though very well intentioned, are like turning the key in the ignition of your car. They light a spark but somehow the engine fails to turn over enough to kick it into action for you to drive off.

Starting a potentially difficult or challenging task is always harder than continuing it. We have been told we will find light at the end of the tunnel and in our heads we sort of believe it. But if we have been avoiding and procrastinating for some time, we experience the feelings of frustration, shame, guilt, tiredness and so on that are so familiar to us and we find it hard to imagine being any other way.

So to use my experience starting this chapter as an example, I have already experienced the lightness, satisfaction and excitement of writing previous chapters and sharing my message with my potential readers because I have a BIG vision to help as many people as I can to travel lighter in their lives. I have felt these wonderful uplifting emotions in my body – so I really KNOW. And yet this time round it still felt like trying to start the car on a cold winter's morning.

In the last chapter we talked about Sarah's experience. Now I would like to share mine.

Victoria's morning

I knew I wanted to write this chapter so I set aside the time, told various people this is what I was going to do and then sat down to start.

Then I got up again.

I remembered I hadn't brushed my teeth – so I went and did that.

I checked my phone and my iPad just one more time.

I sat down again.

I heard the post come through the door so I went to pick it up. Read the postcard from my son in Australia so I sent him a message – just a quick one you understand!

Then I made a cup of tea and drank it. Then a cup of coffee.

Put the cups in the dishwasher.

Went to the local newsagents to buy some stamps as I remembered I had run out and it's a sunny day so a good idea to get out.

In between all this of course I sat down, stood up, turned the heating on, turned it off, opened the window, and closed it trying to get the temperature just right.

You get the picture.

And what did I achieve? Not a lot of anything actually. And what I created were continuing feelings of frustration and discomfort.

And this was because I had temporarily lost sight of the bigger picture. Of the vision I told you about and of my intention to move towards it. I was focusing on the blank page and the time deadline I had set myself, not on what I am in the process of creating and why I want to do it.

As soon as I refocused and got back in touch with this it was much easier to get started and as soon as I did, the sense of possibility and the excitement came back – and the car was on the road again so to speak.

It's the same with handling clutter. You can and you will have a great sense of release and a completely different experience and relationship with your things once you have cleared that clutter. The more you clear and sort out the freer you will be and the more pleasure you will experience.

WHAT WE DO INSTEAD

However if you haven't yet experienced that and are

just being told it, here are some of the things you may find yourself doing instead:

- Small things such as the avoidance tactics I found myself doing that all add up and eat away the time.

- Medium things like putting things out of sight – in the attic, garage or a commercial storage unit.

- Big things like moving house to get more space rather than clearing and making better use of what you have.

- Any of the things that you habitually do which feed the problem rather than addressing it: shopping, bargain hunting, covering it up, anything that gives you a temporary lift.

THE REASONS WE GIVE

These are just some of the things we do and it is essential to RECOGNISE them. (Remember the first part of the ROSE system: RECOGNISE what is really going on).

It is equally important to notice what we are SAYING about what we are doing. Some of the most common reasons we give for not addressing our clutter:

- I haven't the time.

- I'll do it later – when I'm feeling better, the kids have left home…

- There's no point. It'll just come back.

- There's just too much of it.

- It doesn't matter to anybody else.

- I'm too stressed right now.

- I've got too much else on.

- I can't be bothered.

Actually these are not reasons but excuses. A reason would be – I've broken my leg and I'm in hospital. An excuse is really saying 'I am CHOOSING to do something different with my time, I am CHOOSING to avoid taking responsibility and dealing with these issues.'

So just to give you a taste of the shift of state from avoidance and procrastination to excitement and possibility, and to demonstrate to you that getting started is a lot easier than you think, let's JFDI. Just a little bit. Right here and right now. It won't transform your whole life but it will kick start your process.

The 7-Minute Kick Start

Let's take just seven minutes. In that time I invite you to find three things you can do immediately. They will most likely be things to get rid of because of the short time scale. Go with what immediately comes to mind and do it.

To show that you are not alone and to give you examples, this is what I got rid of one time I wanted a quick kick start.

1. A purple biro with a feathery 'cloud' top with a small plane in the middle that lit up. I won it in a raffle on holiday and it used to make me laugh and reminded me of fun times but it was cracked and didn't even work properly. It took longer for me to tell you about it than it did to throw it away!

2. A set of four wooden cats, designed to sit on a shelf edge. I used to have a bit of a thing about cats. These are cute and were a link to my late mother but again they were in the way. Also one of them had been knocked off the shelf and broken its legs about a year ago. I put them in a bag by the front door to be taken to the charity shop later that day. (Not the one with broken legs though.)

3. I removed a significant number of trailing 'babies' from two spider plants. They were trailing messily and inconveniently on the floor so were often a source of irritation and spoilt the look of the main plant.

You might want to make a note of what you got rid of in the margin here.

So the good news is you have started! One step, one bite of the elephant at a time. And that is – or was – the hardest part.

You might find that just those few minutes has really got you enthused and you want to keep going, in which case great – go for it! Everything you make a decision about and act on will move you towards your goal.

But sooner or later you may well find, like I did with writing this chapter, that you hit a bit of a block. And just as I did you will find at that point that the best thing to do is refocus and reconnect with your vision for what you are creating overall.

Obviously if you haven't started by taking the time to create that vision you will have nothing definite to come back to.

So let's focus on how to do that. How to give yourself the biggest kick start possible. It will provide you with solid motivation to come back to if you get knocked off purpose, and the strength to change your excuses for NOT doing something into the reasons TO do it.

START WITH YOUR MIND

You have probably realised by now that the most important place to start this whole process is in your mind. You may have heard the expression 'where attention goes, energy flows'. We are going to deflect the flow of mental energy away from the problems and the excuses and instead turn its full force to the new results you are going to create.

To do this I am going to describe my simple **7-Step Motivational Model**. You may need to read it through a few times to familiarise yourself with it. Then set aside at least 20 minutes and sit down in a quiet place with a notepad and pen to fully engage with it. It will be time very well spent.

7-Step Motivational Model

Step 1: Settle

Take some deep breaths to settle you into the process. Then begin by acknowledging yourself for having made the decision to make positive changes in your life. Recognise and write down some talents and abilities you have that you will bring to this project (e.g. determination, commitment, a creative outlook)

Step 2: Seek

Identify some goals or ambitions you have in relation to the clutter in your life.

Step 3: SMART result

Read through the list and choose one 'hot' result you want to achieve. (Recognise that to make progress we need to break the overall project down to bite-sized chunks so we can repeat this process for each part we identify.)

It is very helpful to use the **SMART** acronym to make the result:

Specific – so you know exactly what you are doing.

Measureable – so you'll know when you've done it.

Achievable – so you are setting yourself up for success, not failure.

Realistic – so you know you can manage the task in that timescale with the resources available.

Time based – so you have a start and/or an end time.

Step 4: So What and Why

List all the reasons you want to achieve this result and why. Ask yourself what you want to experience and what you want to create for your future. Include what you want for the people you live and work with as well as for yourself. Take your time over this and for every 'what?' ask a 'why?'.

Step 5: See and Feel

Put your pen and paper down and close your eyes for this step. Allow yourself to conjure up pictures in your mind of what you intend to create. See the picture as vividly as you can and see yourself in the picture. Try to engage all your senses: See what it looks like to have created this new result – maybe you can hear things or smell things around you and especially feel what it is like. The feelings are as important, if not more important, than what you can see.

Step 6: Specific Actions

From that future you have seen and felt, list all the actions you will take in order to arrive there. Be very specific about each one, making it an identifiable next step. Put a time against each one and make a commitment to take that step.

Step 7: Support

Determine what support you will need to help you through all of this. Decide who you will approach to fulfil this role and when you will do that.

Example:

You might find it helpful to have an example of this model in action so here is an abbreviated example of a previous result of my own:

Victoria's TV room

(Starting from Step 3)

SMART Result:

To convert my TV room into a room suitable and appropriate for receiving coaching clients before an appointment a week away.

So What and Why:

I want to have a welcoming, nurturing and supportive place to see my coaching clients. I want to give them the best possible environment to focus on their growth and development because I care about them and want to give them the best experience I possibly can.

See and Feel:

I had a very clear picture of me and a client sitting comfortably opposite each other in a harmonious space fully focused on our conversation. I could feel the calm and quiet around us and the connection between us.

Specific Actions:

Remove the residual cables from the extra TV speakers and dispose of them.

Remove most of the family photos and find new places for them elsewhere in the house. Also any other family items.

Hang my coaching certificates on the wall in place of one of the pictures.

Set a day and time to do this.

Support:

I told a fellow coach this is what I would be doing and when I was intending to do it and I asked her to hold me accountable.

This final part here, Step 7, is what I call the absolute must have. It's support.

You may be used to doing things on your own, believe you 'have' to do this on your own or just feel you want to (maybe because you are ashamed or embarrassed by the current state of things). But depriving yourself of support is like depriving yourself of food and drink: don't do it.

WHAT DOES SUPPORT LOOK LIKE?

It's having somebody:

- To share your desires and goals with and the belief they are achievable.

- To hold you accountable.

- To watch your back: to catch you if you fall off track and help you get back up again.

- To encourage you to go full on until you complete things and to keep you focused on the task not on stories around it.

- To share your progress and your success.

- To help you handle any emotions which come up.

This last point is particularly important. Clearing your life of clutter can be a very emotional journey. You will need somebody you can call on to help you deal with the sometimes painful emotions that may come up.

How do you choose the right kind of person to support you?

There are certain qualities it is vital to find in anybody you ask to support you here.

To start with, as you may find the work you are about to embark on exposing and feel vulnerable or embarrassed, it is absolutely crucial to find somebody you trust and can rely on. Not least of all to keep confidentiality.

Many of my clients feel very reticent about allowing anybody into what they often see as their hall of shame. They think I can't have seen anything half as bad as theirs. I almost certainly have and I don't judge them for it. It is as it is – and we are going to make it better, together. This is another quality to look for in the person you choose: they must be non-judgemental and focused on the way forward.

You also need somebody who will calmly but firmly keep you to the task in hand. If they keep drifting off, either asking you about the background to things or making numerous cups of tea and taking breaks, progress will be very slow.

This person also needs to be somebody with the ability to be detached. If they find trouble getting rid of things themselves, they are not going to be able to help you clear yours.

Support really is something you must get for yourself and put in place before you get started.

Think who amongst your friends or acquaintances fits this profile, and also seriously consider getting some professional support. It really can make all the difference.

How to use the support

Once you have decided on the person and they have agreed to help, it will serve you both to have a clear agreement as to how you will work together.

It can also be very useful to brief your support person about any ways of behaving or little quirks or tendencies you have that you know might well derail you. Ask him or her to watch out for these and to challenge you to change.

The way I would recommend is the 'do it together' approach where you work physically alongside each other. If this is not possible at all, or only for some of the time, I would highly recommend you set a specific time to share your progress by phone, email, text, whatever suits you.

And at the very end, when the desired result is achieved, make sure to celebrate together and acknowledge everything that has been achieved and all the hurdles that have been overcome.

Remember it can actually be fun to do this. Sharing

laughter will also help you find perspective and lighten the load. And that is hard to do on your own.

SOME FINAL POINTS ABOUT GETTING STARTED

Timing

People often ask 'when is the best time to start?' seeking to get off the starting block at the best possible time. But often they use the issue of time as a means of avoiding taking action: 'It's not the right time' or 'I haven't got the time'.

Recognise that you found the time to acquire the stuff, and you can make the time to clear it. You need to make the handling of it the priority, not the acquiring.

So the answer to the question is now! Now is the best time to start. Even if it is only clearing three things like we did in the short exercise earlier in this chapter.

Now can be anytime – day, night, winter, summer. Especially as most of your physical clutter is probably indoors.

It is also true there are some times when it feels particularly right to get started. In spring for instance, when there is a natural instinct to clear out and clean to welcome the new growth reflected in the natural world. The first of the month or the beginning of the year. (But do beware if you have a pattern of making and breaking New Year's resolutions as that may pose an extra pattern for you to overcome.)

When you have just come back from a trip is a wonderful time to have a new perspective and also some distance from all the things back at base.

But the most motivating thing I have found is to have a compelling event coming up. The most compelling event you will be familiar with is Christmas. And you will know how determined people are to get things done before 25th December.

This does not mean I am recommending Christmas, which can be a very busy time already, I am just giving you an example of how a date can galvanise people into action.

If you don't have a compelling event, I would recommend you create one. Invite friends to stay who will need to sleep in the spare room or on the couch that is piled high with things. Ideally friends who will have to book tickets and make a commitment in their lives so there is extra incentive for them not to cancel.

And if you choose to engage a professional to help you through, you will find the time and money you have committed to spend will go a very long way to making sure you get the very best results.

Prioritise and commit

Once you have decided when you are going to get going on clearing this clutter you really need to make sure you make it a high priority. Blank out the time slot in your diary or calendar. Commit to it and to the result you are going to achieve.

Get organised

Get organised beforehand. Handle anything that really has to be handled. Tell people this is what you are doing and let them know you will not be available during that time. This is very important business and it is not to be interrupted or rescheduled lightly.

YOU CAN DO IT!

Finally, remember you have already started.

Tell yourself:

**It is simple.
It is easy. And most of all know that:
You can do it!**

KEY LEARNING POINTS

- Why getting started can be the hardest part and 'JFDI' just doesn't help.

- How to give yourself a kick start in just seven minutes.

- It all starts with your mind.

- The essential 7-Step Motivational Model.

- The absolute 'must have' is support.

- What support looks like, the best kind of person and how to use them.

- You found time to acquire stuff, you can make the time to clear it.

- Anytime is a good time and certain times are even better.

- 🐘 The importance of prioritising, committing and telling others.

- 🐘 It's simple, it's easy and you can do it!

Tools and Techniques for Things

MY PROVEN TOOLS AND TECHNIQUES FOR ORGANISING THINGS

When we are facing a big undertaking that involves changing our behaviour and our attitudes it can be really helpful to have some good and proven strategies to follow.

I want to share with you my own proven tools and techniques for achieving success. These have evolved over time and I have used them to great effect with many people.

Using the same approach will guarantee your own progress will be easier, faster and overall much smoother. It will also reassure you that as they have worked for many others, they will also work for you. And they will be here for you to refer back to and use again and again if the need should arise.

We are often taught how to acquire things, that having them can make us successful and that we should be polite and accept gifts but nobody taught us how to manage them all and how to make the most of our lives.

Earlier in this book I have mentioned my **ROSE** system:

Recognise

Organise

Systemise

Enjoy!

In the previous chapters I have talked about RECOGNISING what clutter is, the impact it has on us and especially getting in touch with how you want to live instead. By following the exercises you will also by now have recognised specific areas in your own life that you want to declutter.

This chapter is primarily about ORGANISING and sorting your things. It will show you the way to get organised, using simple steps in a systematic way and before you know it, you will find the label on your elephant's neck will read 'not known at this address'.

WHAT TO DO

The first thing we have to do to get organised is – get organised! That might sound paradoxical but what it really means is that some things need to happen on the preparation front. Some of them you have already done by working through exercises in the previous chapters.

You have already:

- Made the commitment to take on your clutter issues and made it a priority.

- Taken the decision to address all those postponed decisions.

- Booked the time – however short or long that may be.

- Created the vision of what you are going to create using the 7-Step Motivational Model.

- Told other people what you are doing.
- Enrolled some support.
- Toured your home or workplace and recognised cluttered areas.

Now you need to:

1. Choose a 'hot' zone.

That is an area that leaps into your mind to be sorted first. It may not be the biggest one but it is one that is having a really niggling effect on you. You may not feel a leap of excitement when you think of tackling it; you may even hear yourself sigh or groan, but this is the place to start.

This is a part of the elephant. It's important not to get distracted by the whole thing or you will just become overwhelmed. It is the area you are going to clear right here, right now. It may be small – just a single drawer or a shelf, or much bigger – say the kitchen. What matters is just to identify one area at a time.

You know the place you need to start. By tuning into the feelings in your body and trusting your gut feeling you will most likely recognise it.

And the most important thing is to get started so if nothing comes to mind immediately just pick one area. It really doesn't matter which. Once you get the ball rolling you will want to continue and you will get to all the others.

2. Organise the hardware

Whatever area you are going to clear first there are some items that you will need and it is advisable to gather them together before you start in order to avoid distraction and delay later on. You will need:

Bags
You will need bags for rubbish and bags for recycling. (The requirements and opportunities for recycling are determined by what is on offer in your area so it is important to check these out beforehand.)

You will also need some bags for items that need to go to other destinations such as to the charity shop or to return to other people. In almost every home I work in my clients have large numbers of often unruly bags particularly plastic bags from supermarkets and large glossy bags from clothes purchases. So obtaining these usually isn't a problem (and using them is part of the solution).

Dusters

Although this is a clearing not a cleaning exercise, you will find clutter is a huge dust trap so you will need some dusters. I also find it particularly useful to have some paper kitchen towel rolls and if possible one of those sprays you mist the leaves of plants with. If you dampen the kitchen towel before you dust with it, the dust will cling rather than being liberated into the air to settle on something else. Then you throw it away - or recycle it. A damp duster will obviously work as well but you will find you get through a lot of them.

Vacuum cleaner

Having a vacuum cleaner nearby is very useful, or one of the miniature dustbusters. But make sure it is not so nearby that you are tripping over it all the time or it will interrupt the flow of the process.

Stationery

You will also need your notepad and a pen handy. Reminders of things you need to do are very likely to pop into your head and it is important to get them out of your head and captured safely for you to attend to later.

A pad of Post-it Notes or some notepaper and sticky tape are very useful. You will find many opportunities to attach a temporary note or label to something.

Camera
A camera is not an essential piece of equipment but it can be a very useful tool to chart your progress. If you have a smartphone the camera on that will be more than adequate.

A skip?
Many of my clients say things to me like, 'I've decided to get my clutter sorted: I'm going to set the weekend aside and hire a skip to throw it all away!'

That is one way of handling your elephant – simply throw the whole thing out and get somebody to take it away. But generally it's not that straight forward and a bite at a time is the only way. You are only likely to need a skip if you are clearing building or garden rubbish.

3. Organise yourself

Having got the materials in place there are some things you can do to get yourself in the right mental and physical zone.

Your clothes
What you wear can help. If you are clearing a big area you are likely to get a bit dusty yourself and you do not want to be worried about your clothes or distracted

because they are uncomfortable, so choose with that in mind.

The colour you choose to wear also has an impact. All colours emit different energies. The colours from the warmer ends of the spectrum – reds, oranges, and yellows will lift your energy so ideally wear these colours – especially on your top half.

Support
Make sure you have your support in place. Either somebody with you or somebody who is holding you accountable. Also make sure you do not have people around who might distract you such as young children. And switch your phone off.

Background
Some people find it energising and helpful to have music playing in the background. Personally I prefer to work quietly but I like to have interludes of loud music to break things up and to have a shake about. If you have any music it needs to have a strong beat – something that makes you want to get up and dance rather than stare out of the window or stop to listen. Electronic dance music is my personal favourite.

Water
It is important to keep hydrated or you will become

tired and lethargic. Keep a glass or bottle of drinking water nearby.

Begin with the end in mind
Immediately before you begin, take a few deep breaths. Look around the area you are about to clear and bring strongly to mind your vision of how it is going to look. This is what you saw when you did the 7-Step Motivational Model. You can even announce aloud your intention to create this. It puts energy and focus into the space and will really make a difference. I can't emphasise enough how vital your mindset is to this process, so choose a positive attitude of decision making and creative change.

HOW TO DO IT

1. Get it all together

In order to organise something we often need to create more disorganisation and even what seems like chaos at the beginning. It is important to see this part of the elephant in its entirety so we can eat it all. So the first thing we have to do is gather it all together.

If you are clearing your wardrobe, for example, you also need to gather together all the clothes that are in the ironing pile, the laundry basket, the mending pile, on the floor and so on.

If it is your desk, find all the piles of bills, half opened letters, correspondence, pens and so on and get them together in one place.

If you are only clearing a single drawer, gather together all the things that would normally be in that one drawer.

We cannot get completely to the bottom of something if parts of it are still out and about. Somehow your subconscious knows there are parts missing that form part of the whole and will not be fully satisfied until all is safely gathered in.

2. The BEFORE photo

Although not essential, it can be really useful to take some 'before' pictures of your clutter. This serves to distance you somewhat from the things and to see them as objects outside of you. It will also show how far you have come when you reach the end and motivate you to live differently in future. It will only take you a minute or two.

3. Organise your piles

Many other books will advise you to have some boxes on hand and label them with the categories you are going to find. Personally I find the boxes themselves get in the way and are never the right shape or size. So my recommendation is to simply designate areas, even just floor space, where you can group related things as you clear.

You can put a sheet of paper or a Post-It Note in each one as a reminder label, but keep your rubbish bag or bin and your recycle bag close at hand at all times. These provide containers for the first category: Things to **CHUCK.**

Then you will need a second area to place items you know you want to keep and **CHERISH.**

The third area will be a holding zone for things you will need to **CHECK BACK** on later. The objective is to keep this down to a very small category compared to the others. Initially you may find it hard to make decisions but once you get in the flow you will not want to postpone any more.

4. Take one bite at a time

As we are very aware now, the only way to eat that elephant is a bite at a time. That is the approach we need to adhere to. And we do it methodically and in sequence. The sequence is to start with whatever is top of the pile or what comes first to hand in the wardrobe and so on, and to deal with that. It is important to avoid cherry picking by going further down the pile and pulling out things we think are easy or otherwise distracting.

So you take the first item, make the decision which pile it goes on – chuck, cherish or check-back. Place it there, and take the next item in sequence. Keep focussed ONLY on the item under decision.

Some items you will immediately know what to do with. When you don't, you will need to ask yourself the right kind of questions. Here they are.

5. Questions to ask yourself

The first question is what I call my Top Tip for Identifying Clutter in Your Life.

If you remember nothing else but this after you have put this book down, I am confident you will have got a good return on your investment of time and money.

So this is how it works: take one thing at a time, look at it or think about it and ask yourself this question:

Does this make my heart SING or my heart SINK?

Literally that is how your body will react: with a heavy dragging down feeling or an uplifting one. An urrrrgh kind of sound or an mmmm one.

The more you ask this question and the more you become familiar with listening to the answer, the easier you will find it to cut to the chase and identify your clutter.

Get used to tuning in to your body and what it is feeling. This is the real clue to your intuition and to what is right for you.

It is also a very important distinction to make that everything that makes your heart 'sing' doesn't have to remain in your life.

So other important questions to ask are:

- Is it fit for purpose?
- Is it genuinely useful to me?
- Do I have enough of this item?
- When did I last use it or wear it?
- Is there a place for it? (Remember there's a place for everything – and it doesn't have to be in your place!)

It's very helpful to remember that William Morris quote too:

'Have nothing in your house that you do not know to be useful, or believe to be beautiful.'

6. Make a decision and act on it

As you listen to the answers to these questions be ruthlessly truthful – trust the first answer that comes to you and – most importantly – act on it.

Put the item in the appropriate pile and move on to the next.

Don't look back and don't allow yourself to dither or

doubt. This is new behaviour you are practising here and although it may be tough at first it will get easier.

As you progress you may very well find you see things that need doing. It is really important to capture these ideas and reminders when they come up so they are out of your head. Don't act on the things there and then but write them down in your notepad and know you will get to them later.

7. Keep going

Step by step, a bite at a time, in an organised sequence. You will get better and faster as you make progress and learn to trust your instincts.

OTHER TOP TIPS TO KEEP YOU ON TRACK

1. Look after yourself

It is very important to take good care of yourself throughout the process of clutter clearing and to keep your energy high so you don't get dragged down by the heavy, cloying energy that surrounds the clutter itself.

Keep yourself hydrated by drinking water at regular intervals. This will also help keep any emotions that come up moving through your body so you can process them and let them go.

Don't neglect food if you are having a long session. Light meals are best as you want to avoid becoming sluggish and tired.

Wash your hands regularly. Not just because they will get pretty mucky but also because the energy of the things will stick (represented in the physical dirt you see) and removing this under running water will also help to keep everything moving forward and not hanging around you. I find I get through lots of hand cream during big sessions as I wash my hands frequently, so that may also be something you want to equip yourself with. (And tissues – a lot of dust gets stirred up too and a lot of sneezing may ensue.)

I mentioned music earlier. To keep your energy high – or to get it back again – it can be a very good idea to put on a piece of high-paced music and have a quick dance or a jump around to change the state you are in. A quick bounce on a rebounder or mini trampoline if you have one is another good idea, as is regularly throwing open the windows (even in winter) for a short while.

As well as breaks for refreshment it can be a very good idea to do little bursts of cleaning. Vacuum out the dusty drawer or corner as you finish it. It will feel a lot fresher and will encourage you to carry on too as you will lighter and freer.

Another way to look after yourself is by putting some boundaries in place. Don't take on responsibility for other people's things. Don't take responsibility for their clutter or things they won't look after for themselves. We will look more into the challenges of other people's clutter later in the book but for now just know it is not your responsibility and your full focus needs to be on your own stuff.

2. Watch your language

Language is vitally important as the fundamental basis of our experience. The words we use create thoughts, the thoughts create beliefs and from there we take actions. Every word that comes out of our mouths and every word used by that ever present chattering voice in our heads to comment and judge has a massive impact on how we behave.

As you proceed with your clutter clearing and meet some of the challenges it will bring up, you need to be very mindful that all the messages you give yourself are positive and affirming.

Be on the constant look out for phrases such as 'I can't… this is difficult… I'll never finish… it's all too much…' and anything similar, and eliminate them completely.

Instead, give yourself constant positive and affirming messages – 'I can do this – and I will. I am in the process of creating an organised and clear space, building the life of my dreams… I am choosing to do this … it's safe to let go and change and I embrace the opportunity…'

3. Ride the roller coaster

You are very likely to experience any important creative project as like being on a roller coaster ride full of ups and downs. This is frequently how it is with clearing your clutter. It is important to recognise this so that you are prepared.

Again I can give a parallel to my process in writing this book: one minute the process is flowing along at a grand pace and I am optimistic, enjoying the process, seeing it as 'easy' and surfing the waves. The next I encounter something I am unsure of or find particularly challenging. Then I may suddenly see the entire thing as too difficult, even impossible, and I'm momentarily off the surfboard floundering around in the water.

The main thing is to keep going and let these feelings pass. Keep momentum and use all the tips I am describing here.

Additionally always focus on what you have done, not what you haven't. Keep going a step at a time and with each one praise yourself for what you have done, however small it may seem, and give yourself constant encouragement.

You will know the saying: 'When the going gets tough, the tough get going'. Remind yourself you are tough and resilient, remember why you are doing this and keep at it.

Taking photos along the way can be fun as well as providing evidence of the progress you are making. If you want to remember something that makes your heart sing but which you recognise is no longer going to have its physical place with you, it is a good tip to take a photo of it and then let it go. This will take up a lot less space than the object itself.

As I mentioned earlier, taking a photo will also help you emotionally detach from the object itself. Letting go of attachment is very important. When you are attached to something you fear to let it go, believing that you will not be fully happy or complete without it.

The reality is you are not reliant on things to make you happy. If you allow yourself to believe you are, you then give your choice and control of your own happiness to those things. And this will prevent you from actually being happy.

Most of our decisions here are made from fear or from love and trust. Most of our acquisitions come from insecurities of one sort or another – fear of not having or being enough.

Any choice made from fear is disempowering. The main reason we procrastinate is fear of making the wrong decision so to avoid that we make no decision at all.

By recognising that these unconscious fears have been a big barrier, you can now choose consciously to be and do differently. You can trust that you are making the right decisions because you are now asking the right questions.

Trust that everything you need in your life is available to you. So ask the questions from a place of appreciation for the love and abundance in your life not from the fear that you don't have enough.

It will also make you more generous towards others. Recognise that something unworn or unused in your wardrobe for instance might be just the right size or thing for somebody else and you can participate in the flow of life by passing it on.

You will experience expanding and uplifting feelings of abundance and gratitude everywhere. You really don't need to surround yourself with things for that.

4. Use the Support!

Finally, don't forget to use your support all along the way. It is very important to have somebody alongside you to keep you steady on the roller coaster. It's like having a hand to hold to give encouragement and help you face all the things I have described here.

WHAT NEXT

1. Complete the session

Taking it a bite at a time and with consistent progress you will get right to the very bottom of the area you are clearing. It is vital to fully complete the session and something many of my clients cite as the best thing about having me work with them. It is so tempting and easy to give up just as the end is in sight. But I keep them to their intention to get the job done. We keep on right down to the last paper clip in the drawer, to grandmother's old lace handkerchief in the cupboard, or the last paintbrush in the garage. We get it out, air it, make a decision about what to do with it and we fully complete the task.

If you don't, you are leaving a little spore of clutter fungus – a tiny baby elephant – just waiting to grow back.

Remember, you need to get right to the bottom of your clutter to get to the top of your game. And that's where you are heading.

So having completely cleared the original area you are left with three piles of things (possibly with sub-piles) that you have decided on next steps for.

The Check-Out pile

Now you have got more practised at letting go you should find this pile easier to deal with. Using the same techniques again, take each item in turn and see what decision you can now make.

If you find you still have things you can't decide upon, put them in a bag or a box and label with the date. Put them away and make a note in your diary to look at them in a month's time. You may well have changed your perspective by then.

The Chuck Pile

A vital thing to do to complete your session is to get the stuff you have decided to let go of out of the house. Of course when I say 'chuck' I do not literally mean put everything in the rubbish, but get stuff away from you as quickly as you can and moved on to the next destination. Put it in the bin, put it out for recycling, take it to the charity shop, or know exactly when you are going to do this – and make it soon. Even putting it in the boot of the car ready to deliver is better than keeping it in the house.

The Cherish Pile

Broadly speaking things in this pile will be of three types: those that you consider the most beautiful, things that are meaningful (to you) and useful things. All these are things to cherish because they greatly enhance your life. And all require and deserve care and attention.

Some things you will be able to find a place for straight away – dust something and put it on the shelf where it can be seen, hang it on the wall and so on. Others may now become projects for the future. Common examples of these are family photographs, household or business paperwork, things stored on now out of date media such as VHS tapes and so forth.

For these you need to make sure everything is collected together and a good temporary storage place is found for it. And be sure to note the project as a To Do item on your list.

You will now have a much better idea of what will be required going forward and anything you might need to acquire such as shelving, an in tray or basket for your mail, some ring binders for your paperwork, decent hangers for your wardrobe and so on. Capture these on a shopping list so you don't have to think back again.

All of this will mean you are finding a place for everything and putting everything in its place – or at least identifying a place you will create. You are now well on the way to becoming organised.

2. The AFTER Photo

Once everything is away and sorted as much as possible at this stage remember to take the 'after' photo, if you have been using your camera. You will be surprised and thrilled at how much you have done and it makes a great full stop on the session.

3. Celebrate

Most importantly give yourself a huge pat on the back. Celebrate your achievements and tell others about it – share your success. You may inspire them to get going on their own clutter too.

4. Moving forward

As you have been clearing, you may well have found that you are going to need to put some systems in place to stop clutter hot spots from building again. We all need systems, however simple, to effectively manage the in and out flow of life and all it brings. For instance you will need a designated place for things that regularly come in and out – mail, catalogues, clean and dirty clothes, even carrier bags!

For now, to complete on the organising part of clearing your clutter you just need to identify these. Setting up a system is a little project and we will be looking at how to handle tasks and projects in the next chapter.

This is the S for SYSTEMISE part of the ROSE system. In case the very thought of it has you running for the hills, don't worry. It is much easier than you might think and the benefits are many.

5. Keep on top – the reality

Clearing out your clutter and organising what is left in appropriate and pleasurable ways, means you actually get to enjoy what is around you in the present moment.

The reality is that things will come and go in your life. It is how you engage with them that will keep you healthy and 'clot' or clutter free.

Having gone through the processes in this book you will be much more aware and make wiser choices about what you choose to bring in and allow to stay. Identifying and cutting off the sources of clutter is the best way to stop it returning. And regularly reviewing your space is the best way to prevent it lingering. This takes diligence and self-discipline but by keeping an eye on the bigger picture of what really matters and what you really value in your life, it will be a lot easier – and you can do it!

KEY LEARNING POINTS

- 🐘 Following a tried and tested approach will make progress easier and faster.

- 🐘 Prepare by getting organised to get organised.

- Identify one part of the elephant, tackle it one bite at a time and Chuck, Cherish or Check-back.

- The right questions will make all the difference, particularly 'Does this make my heart SING or my heart SINK?'

- Looking after yourself is very important – including the language you use.

- Clearing your clutter is like a roller coaster ride – hang on in there!

- Taking photos can be very helpful.

- You are not your things, and things cannot make you truly happy.

- Let go of fear and trust that everything you need in your life is available to you.

- Fully completing the session is very important.

- Keeping clutter free requires diligence and self-discipline.

Unaddressed Issues and Tasks

MY PROVEN TOOLS AND TECHNIQUES FOR ORGANISING UNADDRESSED ISSUES AND TASKS

In the previous chapter we concentrated on how to get organised with Things. I shared with you some simple and proven strategies to follow. These will make your progress easy and fast when dealing with that first category of clutter.

This chapter is about the second category of clutter, Unaddressed Issues and Tasks. In it I will show you how to organise, execute and particularly finish tasks and projects.

One benefit of having this systematic approach to follow is that the process is repeatable. You can learn it first by closely following the steps described here. Then the more you do it the more this way of doing things will become your new pattern. This will enable you to create space, organisation and harmony as a regular way of life.

There are all manner of books, systems and devices targeting the over-worked executive, the busy mum or almost any category of person you can think of. The tools and tips I will outline here will work for everybody who has a task or an issue they haven't yet managed to handle and which is therefore cluttering up their head – and possibly their environment too.

A lot of the principles are the same as for decluttering your things as after all, that is a project too. But again we will take them a step at a time so you can follow easily and move forward to a successfully completed task.

We will start by focusing on the Organise part of my ROSE system. (Recognise, Organise, Systemise, Enjoy!). The main difference will be that we will primarily be organising and dealing with actions rather than objects.

If you started the process of decluttering your life by sorting some things, you may well have identified some projects that are required in order to create your desired living or working environment. I hope you have made a note of these.

You may also have identified the need to systemise some parts of your life to help you manage all your paperwork for example. We will be looking at how to achieve that in more detail.

But first, to give you a taste of where we are heading, I'm going to tell you about one of my clients who I shall call George:

George and his bedroom

George had identified his bedroom as a place that needed attention. It was a mess and didn't reflect how he really wanted to live. He had also recently met a new girlfriend and he wanted to invite her back to his place. He was embarrassed and acutely aware that as he had no coverings at the window she might feel very uncomfortable.

At least a year previously he had purchased a curtain pole and some new curtains. Both of these things had been piled in a corner of the room and become covered in miscellaneous other clutter.

George told me about this at a workshop and together we worked through the 7-Step Motivational Model.

1. *George was pleased he had made the decision to sort his bedroom and said that when he puts his mind to something he really gets it done. He is also quite good at DIY but he didn't have an electric drill of his own. (Settle.)*

2. *He really wanted to make his bedroom a more comfortable and attractive space. He felt the mess and disorganisation was affecting his sleep and there was a lot of frustration tripping over things in the semi dark. He couldn't put the light on at night as people could see in from the street.*

3. *It was easy to see that getting the curtains hung up would be a great start to clearing up the whole room. (Seek.) George determined to get the curtain pole up on the wall and then the curtains on it by the end of the coming weekend. (SMART.)*

4. *We listed all the reasons he wanted to do this. Some examples were to remove sources of frustration and irritation, improve his sleep, to no longer settle for living like that, to create a warm and welcoming place to invite his new girlfriend to, and to make his bedroom private. (So What and Why.)*

5. *In his mind's eye George could see the curtains hanging proudly at the window and feel the clear space where the piles had been. (See and Feel.)*

6. *To achieve this the action list included:*

    - *Call his friend Peter to arrange to borrow an electric drill.*

    - *Remove and sort the clutter on top of the curtains. (Specific Actions.)*

7. *When asked about the drill, his friend Peter had said he would be happy to bring it over to George's place and to help out with the curtain project. He arrived as arranged on Saturday lunchtime.*

> *By early Saturday afternoon they had put the pole up and an hour later had also hung the curtains.*
>
> *They put all the tools, the ladder etc. away and vacuumed the floor, especially where the pile had been as it was very dusty.*
>
> *As an extra, George decided to spend a little while cleaning the windows just to finish the job off properly.*
>
> *They patted each other on the back and stood back and admired their handiwork. They both agreed that actually it had been fun to do and George said how he was now very keen to do more in the room. But for now he had a date to get ready for. (Support.)*

This is a straightforward but very powerful example of how easy it is to follow a process to get something done that we have been avoiding. Now we'll go on to look in more detail at how to do it so you can achieve the same satisfaction as George.

WHAT TO DO

The first thing to do is to choose the task or project you want to address. You will have already done a lot of preparation work for this by working through exercises in the previous chapters.

By doing the exercise in Chapter One, you will have created a list or a mind map of all the unaddressed or incomplete tasks that were in your head – the brain dump.

In Chapter Three you may have already identified the first task from this list that you want to address and used the 7-Step Motivational Model to fully engage with it.

If so, you are already well on the way towards your first goal. If not, let's first look at how to do that part and we'll pick up at point 2 below.

1. Choose a hot project

When you read through your list or look at the mind map you created during Chapter One, you may well find something really stands out for you as the first thing to get handled. That one thing about which you say 'I've been meaning to do that'.

This may not be the biggest or most important task, nor even the most urgent. But you can recognise the annoying and draining effect it is having on you and therefore the benefit of getting it handled.

Don't expect to necessarily feel a leap of excitement when you think of tackling it: you may even hear yourself sigh or groan, but this is the place to start.

Also it is very important to recognise that, especially at the beginning, we want to have an experience of identifying, doing and finishing a task. Once you have experienced that satisfaction and sense of completion you will be motivated and encouraged to tackle more tasks. So the hot project may be one you know you can complete comparatively easily and quickly.

Each project is a mini elephant in its own right. You will have the satisfaction of completing that and also of knowing you have dealt with a bite of the whole bigger picture. As always, the most important thing is to get started, so if nothing leaps out at you immediately just pick the first thing on the list.

2. Use the 7-Step Motivational Model

You can find this model in Chapter Three. It is a key tool for getting tasks done as you have seen from

George's example above. Take time to go through all the steps thoroughly. It will take you a few minutes now but you will more than make up that time when you are carrying out the actions you identify.

Once you have been through all the steps you will have:

1. Acknowledged some of the relevant talents and qualities you bring. (Settle)

2. Identified some tasks you want to address. (Seek)

3. Chosen one result you are committed to handling and defined it very specifically. (SMART)

4. Got deeply in touch with your reasons for doing it. (So What and Why)

5. Explored the vision of what you are going to create. (See and Feel)

6. Made a list of all the specific actions to take and when you will take them. (Specific Actions)

7. Told other people what you are doing and enrolled some support. (Support)

3. The action list

When you wrote your action list it is most likely it just tumbled out in no particular order. This is great as it is vital to get everything out of your head and on to paper. However, you are going to need to prioritise and sequence the actions in order to be most effective. Once you are sure you have them all captured, check to see:

1. If there are any items you need to buy or obtain before you can get started on the task itself.

2. If there is anything you need to do for yourself to prepare (e.g. get childcare in place, or even something as simple as have lunch!).

HOW TO GET THE JOB DONE

1. Review the actions

A lot of actions will naturally have a logical sequence. This will then determine what order you do things in once the basics are in place. If there is no obvious logical sequence you will need to create one. With all of the actions collected together on paper you will be able to see this quite easily.

However, before jumping in and getting on with it, there are three other important questions to ask yourself about each action:

1. Is this action mine and only mine to do?

2. Can I usefully delegate it to somebody else?

3. Does it really need doing in order to complete the task or is it one of those 'it would be nice if…' tasks?

Depending on the answer to these questions you will decide to

DO it
DELEGATE it or
DITCH it

Then you will need to adjust the action list to include any amendments such as potential enrolling and briefing of other people.

2. Begin with the end in mind

Before taking that all important first action step off the starting block, just take a few deep breaths and bring to mind your vision of what you are going to achieve, reminding yourself of how it was when you did the 7-Step Motivational Model. Remember why you are choosing to do this.

You can even announce aloud your intention to handle this task once and for all. You may feel a little self-conscious especially if you are on your own but it will bring extra energy and focus to the task and will really make a difference. Recognising again how crucial your mindset is to the whole process, choose a positive attitude of determination and possibility.

3. Take one bite at a time

Once more remember that the only way to eat that elephant is a bite at a time and this is the approach you need to keep to. Take each action step methodically, following the logical sequence and the priorities you have identified.

If the next action is something you find particularly unpleasant or challenging, just take a deep breath and take it in your stride. It is important to avoid cherry picking by going further down the list and taking actions you think are easy. If you do you will end up with all the most difficult challenges at the end and may find you fall at the last hurdle.

In fact it is a very good idea to do the most unpleasant task first. As long as it makes sense in the sequence, just do it. You will certainly feel better for getting it out of the way.

As you work your way through the actions remember to keep focused only on that one step. However small it may be, give it your 100 per cent attention.

4. Only put next steps on the list

As you progress you may very well find one action generates another. It is really important to capture these when they come up so they are out of your head and you can trust they will get handled. So add them to the list.

I want to emphasise a very important point about actions on that list because it is something we can forget to be clear about when we are in task mode: everything on the list must be an actual action step. Something you can do. So for instance not 'Mum's birthday' but 'Phone company x to get prices of venue hire for Mum's birthday'. That way you will work your way through the list and make progress.

You may also think of actions about other things that need doing. It is important to note these down too, but not to go off and do them right now.

5. Make a decision and act on it

Of course many actions will require decisions. This is one of the reasons you have probably been procrastinating. So remember your commitment is to confront these postponed decisions head on and to move forward. Don't look back and don't allow yourself to dither or doubt. This is new behaviour you are practising here and although it may be tough at first it will get easier.

6. Check in with yourself

As you progress with the actions, make a point of reviewing not only the action list, but also how you are feeling about it all. Get used to tuning in to your body and what you are physically feeling.

Remember the key question to ask when choosing what things to keep in your life:

Does this make my heart SING or my heart SINK?

We can use something similar for checking that our motivation is still strong to keep us going to the end of the task. If your heart is singing you will be storming through the actions; if it is sinking you will be slowing down and finding them particularly challenging. You might even have ground to a halt.

This is particularly likely to occur when you are doing tasks you have identified as things you NEED or HAVE to do. These are most likely to also be the ones you have been shying away from the most, and those you have already started but just can't seem to finish. You can think of no element of pleasure attached to them at all.

If this is the case it is very important to return to the 7-Step Motivational Model exercise, in particular to Step 4 where you have identified all the reasons you want to do this task. As I have said before the mind can be very slippery and subtle in the way it knocks us off course.

You might find on closer examination that you were originally going through the exercise with an underlying 'I don't really want to do this, I'm just going through the motions' or 'This is such a boring/difficult/costly etc. thing but I have to get it done or else… (It'll get worse/my wife or boss won't shut up about it/I'll never get it handled…)'.

The only way to change this is to dig really deep and find some positive reasons you are choosing to do this now. These may be as simple as 'I just want to get it done and out of my mind' or 'I choose to do it because it will make my wife happy and her happiness matters to me' or 'I want the loo to refill quickly so guests can flush it easily and not get embarrassed hanging around in the bathroom for ages' or 'I value my job and I want to do all of it well, even the boring and repetitive parts'.

In this way you reconnect with the bigger picture of why you are doing this and what you intend to achieve.

If you have not put the right kind of support in place for yourself – somebody to really help you get motivated, to hold you accountable and to check in with you, you may well find you flag when things get tough.

7. Keep going

Just keep going: one action step, one bite at a time, in an organised sequence. You will get better and faster as you make progress and experience the thrill of completing that thing you have kept meaning to do and have now actually done.

OTHER TOP TIPS TO KEEP YOU ON TRACK

1. Allow enough time

One of the key reasons we fail to finish a task is that we have under estimated the time it will take. A greetings card I bought recently summed this up beautifully. It was a cartoon of a couple standing beside a ramshackle cottage, with a hole in the roof, drainpipe hanging off, and with a 'Sold' sign outside. The man is saying to the woman 'Don't worry – I'll take a week off work.'!

Think of how many times you have said, 'I'll just do this – it will only take five minutes' and come to realise yet again there doesn't seem to be any such thing as a five-minute job.

Allow as much time as you think you might need – and then add some more. Not so you have more time for delay or indecision but so you have realistic timescales to get the job done all the way to the end.

If you find it impossible to estimate, chunk the tasks down to even smaller bites and do what you can in the time available.

2. Look after yourself

As with anything you do if you only focus on the task and not yourself you will sooner or later find yourself over tired, over hungry, dehydrated and over stretched. It is important to pace yourself and keep your energy high.

Keep yourself hydrated by drinking water at regular intervals and make sure you eat if you are having a long session. Light meals are best as you want to avoid becoming sluggish and tired which will affect your motivation as well as your ability to make decisions and take constructive action.

Remember to keep boundaries in place. If you have delegated a task to somebody else it is important to check in on their progress, but avoid any temptation to take over from them. Trust them to do their bit, as agreed, and express gratitude to them for doing so.

Also watch out for over extending time boundaries. Staying up late at night to get something finished, for example, may be tempting but is more likely to be counterproductive. You may achieve what you want but if you are over tired you are more prone to make mistakes and things will take longer. So recognise your own limits and if necessary renegotiate the time scales with yourself and or others.

3. Watch your language

In the previous chapter I talked about how important it is to be aware of the language you use as you declutter your things. It is the same with anything you do. Try it out on something simple. Say to yourself, 'I **should** mow the lawn'. Then 'I **could** mow the lawn'. And finally 'I **will** mow the lawn'. Notice how the energy and motivation to do anything about the lawn feels different in your body just by changing one word in the sentence.

Other words to watch out for are 'I **have** to...' (e.g. get this finished) which is easily changed to the more empowering 'I **choose** to…' (e.g. get this finished).

As you proceed with your actions watch out for how you might be tripping yourself up just by the words that come out of your mouth.

4. Ride the roller coaster

It is important to recognise that every project will have

its ups and downs as new challenges arise, and motivation can become difficult to sustain. The longer the timescale, the more likely this is to happen.

The main thing is to keep going, keep momentum and use all the tips I am describing. I'll repeat two of the key points from the previous chapter here because they are so very important:

- Always focus on what you have done not what you haven't. Keep going a step at a time and with each one praise yourself for what you have done, however small it may seem, and give yourself constant encouragement.

- Remember the saying 'When the going gets tough, the tough get going'. Remind yourself you are tough and resilient, remember why you are doing this and keep at it.

An extra little tip is to say to yourself the cliché from a popular TV quiz show: 'I've started, so I'll finish'. You have, and you will.

5. Use the Support!

Again I urge you to get some form of outside support throughout. It is so important to have somebody encouraging you, holding you accountable and especially to celebrate your success and achievements with. Friends may feel they cannot challenge you when you fall off purpose and may let you get away with things you are finding difficult. Somebody fully committed to supporting you will keep you moving forward whatever happens and help to make sure you get everything done that you have committed to.

WHAT NEXT

1. Complete the session

So you've got to the end of the project. Ticked the final action off the list and anybody else involved has done that too. But in order to fully complete the task, there may well be some more actions to take that weren't actually on the list. It is vital not to overlook these.

If you have ever had building works done you will have heard of the 'snagging list'. It is a list of all those little but annoying ends of jobs still outstanding when the bulk of a project has finished. The ones that are the hardest to get anybody to come back to complete. People want to move on to shiny new things, and fail to achieve the enormous sense of satisfaction of a job well – and fully – done.

You may have some of those so you must list them and do everything possible to finish them. You may also quite simply need to clear up. Tidy, clean up, pack everything away, and return things to their rightful places – or make a place for them.

2. Celebrate

Give yourself a huge pat on the back and tell others what you have done. Especially those who have been supporting you. Consider what you have achieved – even if it seems only a small thing it is worthy of celebration and a shout of hooray! You can experience as much pleasure from completing a small project or a small part of a larger one, because you have achieved something you wouldn't have done otherwise, and it feels good!

3. Review and prioritise

With the sense of satisfaction and maybe even elation achieved by completely finishing something, you may feel inclined to rest on your laurels. But instead I hope you will be spurred on to do more things on your list.

It is very important to regularly review and update your lists or mind maps. Failing to do this is the quickest way back to feeling overwhelmed. Even if you are not aware of it, your mind will be constantly active trying to hang on to all the things it needs to remember rather than trusting they are all written down in one place and can be referenced at any time. (Make sure you keep your list in a designated place too so you can lay your hands on it easily.)

As you start to tick some tasks off and also get rid of your physical clutter you will find some of your priorities change. You might even have got rid of some potential tasks with the clutter. For instance uncovering a tatty heap of newspaper and magazine clippings of recipes or interesting articles you have been meaning to put in an album, you recognise these are no longer relevant and were never really important enough for you to do anything about. So you let them go. Consequently the project 'Create album of magazine cuttings' needs to be struck off the list.

On the other hand, you might have found that in getting all your paper bank statements together and out of their envelopes you have noticed some things that need addressing. There may well be regular payments coming out of your account you had completely forgotten: rolling donations to charities you no longer wish to support, subscriptions to magazines or journals you never get round to reading, monthly membership of an online dating site you forgot to cancel after you met your partner. It can be quite a surprise to see how much money has been leaking away every month because you haven't been noticing or checking. So a new project could be firstly to review and update all of these bank transactions. This can then be followed by setting up a simple system to regularly check and keep on top of your financial outgoings in the future.

Once all the tasks on your list are current and truly reflective of things you really want to achieve, you need to prioritise them.

Ask yourself 'Where is this issue on a scale of 1 to 10 in my life right now in terms of **importance**?' (1 being 'barely merits attention' and 10 'There is nothing more important in my life right now'.)

Then ask the same question for **urgency.** (1 being 'not urgent at all' and 10 'it has to be done **now'.**)

It will help you to decide what to tackle next and also increase your growing sense of perspective about what really matters to you in your life right now.

SYSTEMISE

As mentioned at the beginning of this chapter, you may well have identified the potential benefit of creating some systems in your life. These may appear as one or more projects on your list. This is the third part of the **ROSE** system – SYSTEMISE – and I want to focus on it here.

You need to set up systems to manage the inevitable in and out flow in your life and to prevent the clutter hot spots and disorganisation and stress from returning.

A system is a way of doing something to improve its efficiency. By setting up an organised, connected series of actions we create a way of doing something that is easily repeatable. Therefore we reproduce the desired outcome deliberately, with full awareness and a lot less effort.

Some systems are very simple to set up – where to keep your keys for example. These are therefore often relatively easy to adapt your behaviour around. Some are more detailed and can take quite a time to get right. Some expert advice and guidance is worth considering – whether through books or by consulting a professional organiser. What is most important is to create a system that works for you. Because if it doesn't, you won't stick to it and you will quickly be back to clutter.

One of the things I do with my clients is to take time to explore what systems – what ways of doing things

— they need in their homes or their offices to make their lives flow more easily. What we create might not always seem logical to other people, but unless those other people are required to work within the system, this really is irrelevant. If it works for the individual concerned, it works. So it is vital to get this right for you.

Managing paperwork is often a big challenge for my clients. It is a project I have undertaken with them many times. I will use the example of a recent client of mine, Laura, to illustrate how this can be done simply. I'll describe the challenges she faced, the actions we took and the results we achieved together.

Laura's challenge

Laura is self-employed, so in addition to the normal household paperwork of bills, voter registration forms, council notifications, letters from the children's schools etc. she has a good deal of records and paper she has to keep together for her tax affairs and other legal and work requirements.

The way she was handling a lot of this was by ignoring it. She would pick up the mail from the doormat and leave it in unopened piles around the house. These were to be found on a very overcrowded desk, on the bookshelves, on top of the microwave, even in the bathroom. She knew she needed to keep a lot of papers so didn't throw any of them out. Every year when her accountant asked her for records and receipts etc. it was a request left unfulfilled till the very last minute. It was finally done with a great deal of stress and anguish, which rubbed off on the other people in the household.

It meant she was regularly late meeting deadlines and incurred unnecessary fines for late submission of essential records. Also, because she was ignoring everything in the post that looked at all official, she missed such things as parking fines and warnings about impending bank overdrafts and charges she could have taken action to avoid. She also missed the good stuff such as cheques clients had sent and even a win on the Premium Bonds. She experienced a constant low level of fear about what might be lurking in the mail and recognised her cycle of avoidance followed by a mad disorganised flurry at the eleventh hour.

Laura's actions:

Laura and I got together at a designated time and

fully focused on her paperwork to get it up to date and to set up a system to manage it for the future.

First of all to get organised we:

- *Gathered together all the piles of mail and papers around her home. Opened all of it; put a lot of it in the recycle bin and the rest in related piles.*

- *Cleared out her filing cabinet. Disposed of lots of out of date papers plus miscellaneous items she had dumped in and on it – including defunct cables, old mobile phones and some old hair tongs (!). Kept only strong undamaged hanging folders.*

Then to set up a system for her we:

- *Designated and clearly labelled file folders for all the categories we had identified during the clear out. These were hung in a simple alphabetical sequence in the drawers.*

- *Set up archive boxes for all the documents she was legally obliged to keep. One for each year so that as a new year starts she can dispose of the oldest year's expired contents and re-label it for the new year.*

- *Agreed a new place for her to put ALL the mail and paperwork that came into the house. We found a basket to act as an in tray that was large enough to contain everything and a convenient place for her to keep it. It was also important she liked the look of it.*

- *Found a pretty box she was happy to have on a shelf near her desk in which she could easily put all her receipts, credit card slips etc. that she needed for her accounts. She recognised that having monthly containers would be ideal but that it was a step too far on the system front for her to maintain, so counterproductive to set up.*

- *Throughout the process I regularly checked with Laura that the systems we were putting in place were achievable for her to maintain and that she could visualise herself doing so easily.*

As the final step, Laura:

- *Committed to: ONLY place mail and related items in the basket; to open it before she put it*

> *in there; dispose of any junk items and see if there was anything urgent; empty the basket completely every weekend and put all the papers away in their proper place.*

Laura's result:

> *When I checked in with Laura a month later she told me she felt liberated. She was amazed to find she was actually enjoying filing things away and being in control of her papers. Her anxiety levels had diminished dramatically and her accountant was thrilled she had been able to find a document he needed quickly and easily – so was she!*

Creating and maintaining simple sustainable systems is clearly the way to a clutter-free life lived and enjoyed in the present moment, as Laura discovered.

This involves making a place for everything and a means for getting it there. Once a system is set up, it can only work with your full commitment to putting and keeping everything in its place on a very regular basis.

You have to work at it to keep on top – but with the right systems in place to suit you and with commitment and some self-discipline you can do it, and you will reap the benefits!

KEY LEARNING POINTS

- 🐘 To finish a project and get the full experience of satisfaction and completion, choose one that is comparatively simple and quick to start with.

- 🐘 Using the 7-Step Motivational Model described in Chapter Three is essential.

- 🐘 Review your actions – Do it, Delegate it or Ditch it.

- 🐘 Your mindset is vital: begin with the end in mind and move towards it one action step at a time.

- 🐘 Only put specific actions on the list, not topics.

- 🐘 Be realistic about timescales.

- 🐘 Look after yourself and watch your language as your actions and your motivation may ebb and flow.

- 🐘 It is very important to fully complete the project – including any 'snagging list' jobs and clearing up.

- 🐘 Regularly reviewing and prioritising your To Do list will keep everything in your life up to date.

- 🐘 Creating and maintaining simple sustainable systems that work for YOU is a crucial part of a clutter free life.

The Head and the Heart Part

MY PROVEN TOOLS AND TECHNIQUES FOR MENTAL AND EMOTIONAL ISSUES

After Things, and Unaddressed Issues and Tasks, the third category of clutter I have identified is Mental and Emotional Issues. This is arguably the most significant of all because it lies at the root of everything.

Every day when we wake the little voice in our head leaps into action and starts its non-stop commentary on literally everything. Mostly we don't notice it at all. We are so used to it we simply blank it out, and a great deal of it is unconscious. Some people talk to themselves out loud so are aware of some kind of dialogue with themselves, but not of the full depth and intensity of what is going on inside.

When all is said and done any object – a plate, a pair of earrings, an old teddy bear – is just that. An object. It is not your grandma, your lover or the only source of comfort and solace in your life. And if a friend disagrees with something you said it does not automatically mean she doesn't like you, and you can't have her as a friend any more.

We endow things with significance and meaning and place our own interpretations on events, often unconsciously. All these add up to become our life's story and some of the interpretations serve us and some don't. The challenge is to sort out which is which.

WHAT'S BOTHERING YOU AND WHAT TO DO ABOUT IT

Back in Chapter One I invited you to take the time to engage with some questions to uncover and write down things you would describe as currently bothering you and therefore distracting you and causing you stress and anxiety.

Now you have brought these things to mind, you can choose to do something about them.

Option A - action

Recognising that something is an issue for you could be enough motivation to just get on and address it. Or you might find the 7-Step Motivational Model described in Chapter Three, and regularly referred to throughout this book, is appropriate and helpful.

Some steps of the model might need some slight adjustment for this. The result you want to create might be for instance to reconnect with somebody you have had a falling out with. Perhaps there is an apology you now want to offer, or some amends to make.

It will be necessary to look carefully at the steps of the process if this is to involve somebody else. We can only be responsible for our own actions and commitment so the final outcome is less predictable. Consequently some slight modifications may be required.

Option B – avoid

On the other hand the thing you may choose to do of course is to ignore and avoid the issue. This is when we usually start making excuses and inventing reasons. First to ourselves and then to other people. Then we find ourselves acting from these excuses and behaving in different ways: we cross the street to avoid somebody we have had a previous altercation with or we don't answer the phone when we know it is them calling.

We justify our own behaviour by making ourselves right and the other person wrong and consequently see the issue as something they have to do something about, not us. That's a great way to avoid doing anything – make it somebody else's responsibility.

Very often we REACT to situations in our lives from habitual and old patterns. When this is happening we are not open to RESPOND to circumstances in new and more creative ways. We might know we want to change but keep falling back into old familiar patterns.

It is always mental and emotional issues that will halt us in our path. These issues will rear their heads whether it is a specific emotional issue we are already dealing with or an object or a task that is triggering emotions.

Emotions are always present, even if we don't notice them. Recognising and dealing with our own emotional clutter will deliver us to exciting new challenges and ways of being.

HOW TO RECOGNISE A DERAILMENT

When you created your list of mental and emotional clutter in Chapter One, I encouraged you to maintain emotional distance from the actual issues. I also suggested that you observe as much as possible with an intention to identify and uncover your own patterns.

These patterns will be messages you habitually tell yourself such as 'I'm really clumsy, others are more intelligent than me, I always say the wrong things'. And they will also most importantly be what you do.

So focusing specifically on the clutter issues and how you handle them, it is extremely useful to notice the things that trip you up and prevent you moving on. They stem from obstacles in your head, which become pitfalls to trap you and rabbit holes for you to dive down. The result is that you are derailed from your purpose and you never get to achieve what you set out to.

Using all the tools and techniques in this book may be more than enough in many situations to inspire and motivate you to get to the very bottom of your cluttered area and the very end of your project.

However, as I have previously described, clearing any sort of clutter is a roller coaster ride and many opportunities will arise for avoidance and procrastination along the way. You need to make sure anything that delays or prevents you completing the task when you said you would is a valid reason and not just an excuse.

It is a normal and understandable human reaction for us to look for ways to bail out when we come up against difficult emotions in order to protect ourselves from experiencing them.

How do you know if this is happening to you? It is quite simple: you recognise you are no longer doing what you said you would.

Instead you are doing any number of other things. These are usually things which give you pleasure at least temporarily, and take you away from the painful emotions that are surfacing which you haven't noticed.

Jonathan's story

A client of mine called to book a session to help him clear his late parents' effects. It transpired this was arranged for a day when Test Match cricket was on television and he was a cricket fanatic. He had failed to mention this to me in advance and not having any interest in cricket myself, I was unaware of the importance of that day's events on the pitch.

We struggled to keep him on task and away from the television throughout the day so progress was slow and frustrating. I had assumed the timing was an accident, but the second time he asked for an appointment on a cricket day (I checked!) I saw the pattern, and we scheduled an alternative day.

On the second occasion, although he came up against difficult emotions around his parents' passing, we were able to move through these together and we got the task done. He was then able to watch the cricket on another day with full and undivided attention. He enjoyed himself much more and also had the satisfaction of having completed something that had been bothering him for a very long time.

We can be very subtle and sophisticated in finding ways to protect ourselves from what we anticipate is going to be painful. We often need somebody else to help us recognise this and to support us through the situation rather than trying to go round it.

The good news is that because this is SELF-sabotage, we can recognise it and the power to do something different lies in our own hands.

HOW TO RECOGNISE THE DRIVER

Emotions are a natural part of life and they are intended to flow freely through our bodies then dissolve once they have been fully experienced. As children, however, we are often taught that certain emotions are not socially acceptable (anger and sadness feature highly here – sometimes even joy and excitement too). So we learn to suppress them and in time become even unaware of them.

These blocked emotions can become toxic clutter in our bodies – the clot I was talking about in Chapter One. This is sometimes described as emotional baggage and we somehow seem to think it is fine to accept that we collect more of it as we grow older. We fail to recognise the impact of carrying it around with us.

We tell our stories of real or imagined hurts inflicted on us and justify our own bad behaviour towards others. As we keep repeating these stories we get to relive the pain and the outrage. It goes deeper into our psyche and our bodies. It festers there and takes its toll on both our mental and physical health. It also serves to keep us stuck in our lives, often seeing ourselves as powerless victims of circumstances or of other people.

If we don't allow ourselves to express anger, for instance, it doesn't go away, it just gets suppressed. Then something will happen that may just be a tiny little thing on its own but on top of all the other anger it is enough to tip your emotions over into a full scale explosion.

However, anger is not the emotion in the driving seat when we get derailed from our decluttering. It is fear. Fear of making a wrong decision, fear of change, fear of being judged and criticised.

When your body registers an emotion there is a corresponding physical sensation. These are our feelings – so named because we literally feel them in our body. You may manage to hide from yourself this is what is happening through unawareness or learnt behaviour but your body will register it whether you recognise it or not.

Some of the feelings of fear manifest themselves as tightness, cramps, shaking, and sweating. You may withdraw into yourself or become irritable, listless or restless.

This is why you will find you want to get away from the issue that has brought up those feelings and do anything rather than face the fear. Watch the Test Match; have a cup of tea (or maybe a glass of wine); feel suddenly very tired and tell yourself you simply can't go on without a lie down.

I call such displacement activities your 'Get out of Jail Free card'. It is like a ticket you give yourself to make it OK to avoid something and to create an excuse. Instead of stopping to ask yourself: does this action I am about to do further the task in hand or is it a rabbit hole I am about to go down you just do it.

Take a moment to reflect on which ones you have used. Maybe you stay in bed too long, find things in the house that just can't wait, get engrossed in magazines or articles you haven't bothered with before, remember something you have to go out and buy or do, somebody you just have to call, emails you *have* to check, Facebook, anything.

We are so familiar with these ways of behaving it does take courage and curiosity to stop and reflect on what is underneath some of it and to face the fear instead of running away from it. That can be the biggest challenge and can also deliver the biggest results.

WHAT TO DO ABOUT IT

Tamara's trousers

I bumped into a former client recently. She said, 'you'll be really proud of me – I cleared out 12 pairs of trousers at the weekend!'

I had worked on other areas of her house with her but not on her wardrobe. However, she had been so enthused and excited by the work we had started together she was now working her way through the whole house.

She continued, 'I hadn't done it before because I realised I was afraid I wouldn't have anything to wear to work if I threw out any of my trousers.

'But when I went through them one at a time I saw I didn't wear any of these anyway – ever. They were just sitting there in the wardrobe taking up space and making it hard to put anything away or to see what else was in there. So I bit the bullet and took them all to the charity shop on Saturday afternoon. I even discovered that behind them were a couple of favourite tops I thought I had lost, which was a bonus.

> *'I realised the fear was ridiculous and unfounded but had been stopping me doing this till now. I still have more than enough to wear to work and I love my new wardrobe space. What was all that about? Just a waste of time and very frustrating!'*

Tamara had been on a roll with her clutter clearing. When she came up against this obstacle, instead of just putting everything back in the wardrobe and walking away, perhaps to find something easier to clear, she stopped to check what she was feeling and saw it for what it was – an irrational fear of not having enough for any and every eventuality.

Tamara's actions demonstrate beautifully the two requirements we need to release our emotional repression. First to be open to the feelings, then to accept them. Once we can acknowledge the fear that is blocking us we can remind ourselves of all the many higher reasons we want to handle this issue and choose to let the fear go and do it anyway.

Emotional Spring Cleaning

Although fear is undoubtedly the biggest emotional block, there will be other emotions present too, such as guilt or frustration, and it is equally important to recognise them. A little exercise of emotional spring cleaning will really help you with this, so here is how to do it:

Emotional Spring Clean

- *Notice where you are feeling discomfort in your body, especially where this is accompanied by a strong desire to push the feeling away.*

- *Close your eyes, and take some slow deep breaths into the part of your body where you feel the emotion most strongly.*

- *Be open to the feelings and try your best to name them. Accept they are there and allow yourself to experience them.*

- *Instead of judging yourself for having these feelings or trying to change them, be compassionate to yourself and recognise the complexity of human emotions.*

- *Choose to stay with the feeling, breathing deeply and keeping your attention on it. Then notice how it becomes less intense and actually begins to move through you.*

> - *Bring any issue to mind that you are dealing with and see if other feelings are now present – such as courage to make changes, excitement at new possibilities.*
>
> - *Be grateful for the ebb and flow of emotions in your body for this is a rich experience of being fully alive.*

It is so important to acknowledge your feelings to yourself. By telling yourself the truth about them and about the issues you are confronting you will strengthen your motivation and determination to make changes and move forward.

You are acknowledging the presence of the fear but not allowing it to take over. Instead you can reiterate your intention to do whatever you have committed to even if you are afraid and tempted to avoid it. You might even recognise that the fear is signalling a great opportunity for growth and change and that could help your motivation too.

Other people

We do not exist in isolation and you will find your emotional clutter issues will often involve other people. It makes for increased challenges when we come head to head with other people's clutter in whatever shape or form. So it is vital to get on top of your own issues first.

If you are not confident with your own beliefs, your own sense of self and of your own motivation you are likely to look to other people to provide this for you. This will generate more fear and confusion as to what you really want and what is really true for you. Your own fear of not being good enough, for example, is projected out onto others with the unconscious fear they will judge you and find you wanting.

If you are confident that what you want to produce for yourself is, for example, a highly organised filing system then you will get on and do it. If you are not so sure and somebody scoffs at the suggestion and calls you anal or obsessive you are not going to do it.

Once you have a perspective on your fear it will fuel your self-confidence and self-belief. You will know what you want and have complete trust that you can handle it. To quote the title of the late Susan Jeffers' groundbreaking book you will be able to *Feel the Fear and Do It Anyway*.

So you may lay yourself open to being judged by other people, but the other side of the coin is that you judge them too.

You may judge them for not handling their own clutter issues for instance and blame them for messing up your life and your home or office. You may blame them or use them as your excuse for not handling your own issues.

Recognise that this may well be one of your Get out of Jail Free cards – passing the buck of responsibility.

Other people's clutter

On the other hand, other people's clutter is a very real issue when it is in a shared space such as a home or office. Remember there are three options to getting things done here: they do it alone, you do it together or you do it for them.

In this case, unless they are already highly motivated to clear their own clutter (give them this book and see if that helps!) it's not going to happen. You may be able to do it together but the challenge for you will be to allow them their own experience and avoid telling them how they should be. Or you can do it for them. This may seem the easiest and quickest way to make things better and it will look like that at first. But pretty soon the clutter will be back to how it was and you may have caused bad feeling and resistance in the process.

All you can do in these circumstances is to do your own work and lead by example. Trust that the energy released and the great positive changes you make will be infectious and the other person will want to get going too.

There is however one category of other people's clutter which might well fall to you to sort at some point and that is following a death. Though of course strictly speaking at that point they are no longer the deceased person's things – they have become yours to sort.

There are many tips and pertinent points about this throughout the book but as this is the place we are looking at emotional issues there is something I want to mention specifically.

Following any bereavement there will inevitably be a period of intense grief. There is no telling how long this will last as it is unique to everybody. Emotions are fresh and raw and dealing with the deceased's belongings in the early days may prove too much for some people to handle.

All the principles outlined in this book are just as valid but an extra degree of compassion and care is called for in such circumstances. It is particularly important to remember that the things are not the person and by letting go of these you in no way diminish your connection to them. And keep an eye as always on what you want in your life now.

MOVING FORWARD

Early one Friday evening a while ago I was on a crowded train heading out of London. I happened to sit next to two smartly dressed young men who had clearly just been on some kind of business management training course. As one of them got off the train at his stop he turned to his companion and said, 'See you on Monday. Come with focus not with fear!' They both laughed and I laughed to myself too. It seemed such funny management speak.

But actually it is a really useful phrase and I have never forgotten it. It's not that the fear isn't present but it is the focus that makes the difference and that is what I am emphasising here.

So let's focus on your 'Monday', on the issues you will be facing as you address your clutter issues. Let's summarise some of the ways of behaving that you will need to change. These will enable you to stop dwelling on the past and speculating fruitlessly on what if's and how things could or should have been.

You can't start the next chapter of your life if you keep re-reading the last one. Focus on what you want to create in the today that you have and the future you are moving towards. Make your intention to do whatever it takes to get on top of your clutter, to stop procrastinating and postponing decisions.

And along the way it will really benefit you to:

STOP and let go of:
- Blaming.
- Complaining.
- Criticising and judging.
- Fear that blocks you.
- Making excuses.
- Passing the buck.
- Re-telling stories.
- Trying to control others.
- Worrying what others might think.
- Worrying generally.

START to embrace:

- Being kind to yourself in thoughts, words and actions.

- Being kind to others.

- Change – nothing lasts for ever.

- Choosing a positive attitude and a creative outlook.

- Exploring and finding your true purpose in life.

- Knowing one small change can make a massive difference.

- Opportunities for new and better things in your life.

- Taking full responsibility for what is yours.

As a final illustration I'm going to tell you about:

Angela's attic

Angela is a talented and creative artist who works with textiles to create beautiful garments, jewellery and pictures. She has a studio in the attic room of her home. Before I met her she had been experiencing a lot of frustration, together with a lack of energy and enthusiasm and had produced very little work for quite some time.

The area of her studio she could actually work in had shrunk to almost nothing. She wanted to do something about this but was frightened to get rid of anything to free up space. She was stuck and anxious because she was frightened that she would later regret anything she did get rid of because she might need it in the future. Also she had spent a lot of money on fabrics and threads and believed if she were to give any away it would be like pouring money down the drain.

She had asked all her friends what she should do and sought reassurance from them. Of course, some said, 'just clear it out and let it go', and others merely reinforced her fears by saying things like, 'you can't possibly get rid of those beautiful things and anyway you might need them sometime'.

As a result of our talks she told some truths: what she wanted was more space in her studio; she couldn't achieve that without getting rid of some things; and if she couldn't see or reach her materials she couldn't and wouldn't be using them anyway.

She knew absolutely that the lack of space was stifling her creativity. She recognised her fears around letting go but also recognised she could get help with this. She also knew there were some fabrics she had simply got tired of. She could either sell them or give them away and get the relief of clearing them from her own space coupled with the pleasure of giving them to somebody who would use them and give them new life.

With this clarity and motivation she sorted through her shelves and drawers. She was able to discern what materials really inspired her and reignited her creative passion and energy and the rest she let go.

KEY LEARNING POINTS

- Things are not people and you can choose the meanings you attach to them.

- When you avoid something you make excuses to justify your choice.

- You REACT from old habits and beliefs, you RESPOND from truth and clarity.

- You get derailed from your purpose when unpleasant emotions arise that you want to avoid.

- Blocked emotions and emotional baggage affect health and well-being.

- Diversionary tactics help to avoid the pain but only give us temporary pleasure.

- You need to allow yourself to acknowledge and experience the full range of your emotions and they will pass.

- *Feel the Fear and Do It Anyway* is the only way through.

- You cannot handle other people's clutter for them if the process is to have any lasting result.

- Bereavement and things that need sorting after a death present particularly sensitive challenges.

- Stopping old attitudes and ways of being and embracing new positive outlooks will take you to the next chapter of your life.

Delight at the End of the Tunnel

WHY IT'S IMPORTANT TO KEEP ON TOP

A roller coaster ride, a journey through a long dark tunnel, whatever the process of clearing clutter from your life may seem like to you, you will reach a point when you feel you have arrived at your destination. By following the proven systems described in this book you will come through the challenging times and reach the daylight. You will experience more energy, satisfaction and a great sense of travelling lighter. This will be the case whatever type of clutter you have been working on.

One of the favourite books I read with my children when they were small was *A Clean House for Mole and*

Mouse by Harriet Ziefert. The story is very simple and describes what the animals did throughout a whole day to get their home spic and span. By the evening they were very happy but so exhausted they couldn't bear to go inside and have some food as it would make the house messy again. So they had a picnic in the garden.

Even if you are tempted to do something similar and avoid the areas you have cleared of clutter to avoid messing them up again, this is unrealistic. It is important to fully experience the sense of achievement, take the after photos and give yourself a big pat on the back. And it is also very important to recognise this is the beginning of another way of living your life and it is going to take some getting used to.

The vision you have of how you want your life to be on an on-going basis really matters and it is achievable. You have worked hard to get things organised and addressed and now you want to keep them that way by embracing the process not by avoiding it.

One reason to keep on top in your new life is of course to stop things returning to the clutter-filled, disorganised, stressful way they were before. In Chapter Two I described different ways we become motivated and said that doing something because it takes us away from pain does work but only until the worst of the pain has gone. On the other hand, doing something that delivers us pleasure is something we want to keep doing.

Having experienced some of the delights and pleasures of clearing clutter you will find you want more of it. You will also want to carry it forward and relish the challenges and the new behaviours of keeping your life that way: living what was once a dream of how it might be but now is a reality. So these are the most significant reasons to do what it takes to keep on top.

The good news is that keeping on top of your clutter is a lot easier than all the clearing and sorting and completing you have been through, and a lot less stressful than getting started in the first place.

As an example of this, let's look at:

Carol and Martin's story

Carol and Martin had lived in their delightful cottage for almost 30 years and raised two children there. They had recently undertaken substantial building works to extend their kitchen, the heart of their home. Everything in the house had been in a state of upheaval – and although the builders had left a while ago things had never really returned to the sense of peace and order the couple craved.

Before we met I had encouraged them to take a good long objective and dispassionate look round their home: to ask themselves what they would like to change, what they would like to see and how they would like to feel there.

Both had made lists on their phones so they could add to them at any time.

They both identified the bedroom as having the most impact on them so our consultation focused on that. By seeing the room in bite sized chunks we were able to clear away the unused trouser press, the old TV moved upstairs during the building works and subsequently replaced, magazines, all the hanging and shelf space in the two wardrobes. Finally the plastic bags of stored but unwanted old pillows and the 'we wondered where that had gone' family silver teapot were found all crammed together on the top of the wardrobe.

Because we had identified these specific areas we were able to tackle them one at a time with an increasing sense of progress, achievement – and delight.

I left them with clearly defined next steps to be tackled on their next day off work: the top of the dressing table and the pile of paperwork on a chair. They were so enthused by the sense of exhilaration and relief to have started and already made a substantial difference that they carried on the momentum over the following weeks and went through the entire house. They ticked items off their lists as they went, celebrated their success and kept the cleared areas free and easy to clean.

Only a month after my visit I received an email from Carol:

I just had to tell you I have now sorted all the paperwork out – very liberating! I have also sorted all our photos and the linen cupboard. It feels so good… Also now when I go shopping I ask myself, first do I need it but most of all, have I got a place for it?

Martin is wonderful; he is doing the same thing with other things.

Then the best and most important exercise was decluttering my day, week, month so now I have more time for fun things.

WHAT IT MIGHT TAKE

Carol and Martin were motivated to keep going because they were reaping the benefits of their clearing and enjoying living differently. They kept taking time to stand back and look at what was still cluttering up their lives and distracting them from doing what they *really* wanted, including having the space and time to invite friends round to their newly extended home.

Let's look at what else is required to keep our lives clutter free:

Regular reviews

Just as Carol and Martin did, it is important to regularly take stock. To review the things you have around you and see if they truly reflect how you want to be right now. Check what issues are bothering you that you might have swept under the carpet and what tasks you may have been avoiding. Look at your current health and stress levels and see what is affecting these for good or ill. How are you now spending your time? Are you doing the new hobby you wanted to? If not, why not?

Carol and Martin were doing this very regularly while they were getting on top and clearing the bulk of things, but as it becomes more of a habit just one major review of your clutter a year may be enough.

Easy systems

The easier and more suitable any system you have put in place is, the easier it will be to handle. If your system doesn't work, change it to one that does – quickly.

Commitment and self-discipline

For any system to work you have to use it consistently. You need to commit to this and also to deal with things as they arise. This may be as simple as writing something down on your list, but it is extraordinary how much effort it can sometimes seem to take just to do that one simple thing. You may delay but time and life won't, so you will soon be back to a cluttered head with things forgotten or overlooked. Make a commitment to do what it takes and exercise the self-discipline to carry it out. Cultivate a zero procrastination mindset. It can actually be fun to challenge yourself and to change your behaviour.

Carol's email also mentions an arena in which self-discipline and new behaviour may often be required: shopping. Her questions were 'do I need it?' and 'do I have a place for it?' These will make you stop before making a purchase and help you to cultivate increased awareness and more conscious choices around the things you buy and what you spend your time doing.

Personal responsibility

It is very important to recognise what our part is in creating any environment or relationship. We live in an increasingly blame culture: anything we don't want or like we see as somebody else's fault and we abdicate any responsibility.

A small example of this happened in my aunt's house when the family cat had her kittens in my cousin's trousers. He had let them fall on the floor when he took them off and left them there for a couple of days as he often did. When he woke one morning he found they had become a nest for the cat and her three beautiful newborn kittens. He was furious with the cat and blamed her for ruining his trousers. He couldn't see that all she had done was to find a warm and comfortable place to give birth and that if he had taken responsibility to put his trousers away in the cupboard it couldn't have happened.

In this case my cousin's argument was with the cat but more often things we fail to take responsibility for can become a source of conflict with the people around us.

Try to avoid arguments about it: don't leap to defend yourself or retaliate by heaping blame on the other person. Instead listen to what they have to say with open curiosity and see this as useful feedback of things you might not have seen before, and as an opportunity to do things differently.

Co-operation

We might achieve harmony in our environment but it won't feel that harmonious if we are not doing the same in our relationships, particularly with the people with whom we share that environment.

A sense of perspective is very helpful here. What bothers you might be a picture hanging crooked; what bothers them might be your pile of papers on the chair where they want to sit. Recognise that we all have different ways of seeing things, and some acceptance and compromise will make for more harmony.

An even better thing to aim for is 'creative co-operation' (a term identified by Stephen Covey in his book *The Seven Habits of Highly Effective People*).

Carol and Martin were great examples of creative co-operation. With their newly organised and systemised home, they realised they would require clarification and new agreements about things such as no more piles of paper on chairs or sports shoes by the front door. They agreed that each person would be responsible for putting their own things away and for returning household items to the right place.

They found new ways of doing things they were both willing to do, because the bigger picture was a harmonious home and harmony between everybody in it.

Planning ahead

Reviewing is really taking stock of where you have come from and where you are now. In conjunction with that it is necessary to look ahead and see what could or will come up to require your time and attention.

You may be able to anticipate possible causes of anxiety and clutter in your head. You may be planning a big event for instance, so it is worth taking some time well in advance to plan your approach. Recognise your wants and desires but also your limitations. Then you can decide whether to go for the Do It Alone, Do It Together or Done For You approach and put things in place to get organised.

Legacy

This is the ultimate area in which planning ahead can benefit not only you in the here and now, but your nearest and dearest in the future.

All of us are only passing through life. We come into it as into the middle of a movie and we have to come to terms with leaving before the end. By paying some time and attention to the question of your legacy you will be taking responsibility for your life in the fullest sense.

Anything we have, however glossy and expensive or small and cheap is only ours for our lifetime. And it really is a truism that you can't take it with you when you go.

Actually it is an illusion to think we really possess anything. We might have the title deeds or the receipt but stuff happens to things – accidents, theft, wear and tear and they disappear. That said, there is usually still quite a lot hanging around once we reach our middle of the movie or curtain call. If we haven't taken responsibility to sort and take care of it all while it was in our possession, somebody else will have to sooner or later.

Some people say this doesn't bother them. That it's fine, it'll be somebody else's problem. Others write and rewrite wills in an attempt to control things from the grave. Once more a perspective is required here but at the highest level I would say that any will is better than no will.

You might think it is easier not to address this topic, because it's maudlin or tempting fate and to continue with the illusion that it (death) won't happen to you, or at least not for ages. But this will also be a source of clutter in your mind, however deeply pushed down and avoided. It is something you know you should do something about as a responsible adult.

So if you haven't, I strongly urge you to do something about it right now. Pick up the phone and call a solicitor to make an appointment, look online at other options available and choose one, or go to a stationer and buy a write your own will kit. Or at least make one of these a priority on your To Do list. If you have already made a will, make reviewing it a part of your annual life review as suggested above, because circumstances and preferences do change.

HOW TO KEEP ON TOP

Use the ROSE system

The best way to keep on top and therefore to live with the delight at the end of the tunnel is to use the **ROSE** system I have been detailing at points throughout this book.

In so many areas it is important to:

RECOGNISE what is really going on.

ORGANISE your things and your mindset.

SYSTEMISE whatever you can to make things easy and repeatable.

ENJOY living a harmonious life happily connected to your things and to the people around you.

I encourage you to make these the four cornerstones of your life. They encompass my proven systems for getting everything in your life up to date and how to keep it that way.

There are some final tips I want to share here with you.

Get it all together

The mention of legacy is a very good prompt to recommend you make a list of your financial affairs: bank accounts, investments, any Post Office savings together with account details. You never know what you might uncover by doing so: a forgotten policy, or a dormant account with money still in it. This is a great way to declutter and to get your life in order. By leaving all these details in a safe place, you will be leaving a system for your beneficiaries that will help them at a difficult time.

You are also giving your children or others around you a great example of how to take responsibility for their own affairs and keep them in order.

Take care of your things

As well as your finances you may have other things that would benefit from proper care.

Elizabeth's wine cellar

A widowed client of mine had inherited a large amount of valuable and specialist wines when her husband died unexpectedly. She had moved house after his death and taken it all with her, but as she no longer had a cellar to keep all the bottles in they were stacked in conditions very ill-suited to the products and actually detrimental to their quality and value.

With prompting and encouragement she recognised that this was now her collection and no longer his and it would honour her husband's memory more by looking after and enjoying the collection he had created than allowing it to spoil. She contacted a very expensive restaurant in her area and eventually came to an arrangement whereby they would rent her some storage space in their very large cellars in exchange for a couple of cases of the wine which they would put on their list as a very specialist buy for people dining with them.

The message here is don't let things build up. One small change, one small action like a phone call can make a big difference and start a whole new ball rolling for you.

Declutter your diary

Decluttering your diary is also a very rich exercise, as mentioned by Carol in her email. Choose to spend your time how you really want to. And if there are things in there because they have to be or need to be attended, think how you can change your attitude to make doing them a positive choice.

Learn to say No

Learning to say no is another muscle you may need to work on. Thank you but no, I'm not available on Wednesday (you don't have to explain why).

You might also need to practise saying no to yourself. No to the attraction of things proclaiming loudly they are bargains/free/new/the latest thing. Remember you are not saving money you are actually spending on things you hadn't planned for and don't need. You might get a momentary high by acquiring what has cleverly been marketed as a bargain. But you may well also suffer buyer's remorse later and wonder what on earth possessed you.

Just because something is free doesn't mean it deserves house room at your address. (Goodie bags from planes, beauty cosmetic counters and similar are particular attractions for you to practise saying no to.)

You might well find the hobby of shopping is no longer so appealing if you are not buying. So my suggestion is to cultivate the approach of enjoying looking but without the need to buy. You can enjoy things without owning them all. Remember, however big or expensive the purchase, if we are buying for buying's sake the gloss will soon fade and you will want more – bigger – newer. You will also be sending messages to your children that this is the way to find happiness. Except it isn't for long – only while the 'fix' lasts.

Learn to say Yes

When we tell ourselves no the message we can get is of deprivation, so the top tip here is to say yes to yourself. Yes to positive choices that will keep your life free of clutter, yes to maintaining a detached curiosity about your behaviour – how it was before and what different choices you are making now.

If you find you are behaving in old familiar ways you can even say yes to that. Don't beat yourself up or become obsessive. You are on a journey towards a clutter-free life, and the odd transgression will not take you from that as long as you keep your sights on the bigger picture.

ENJOY!

The final part of the **ROSE** system – and the reason we do any of it is to ENJOY ourselves more. I really believe life is to be enjoyed not endured.

It is my most sincere hope that you will have read this far and found freedom and pleasure from clearing some clutter from your life. Even doing the 7-Minute Kick Start exercise to clear out just three things as suggested in Chapter Three may have made a difference.

However much of an issue resolving your clutter has been for you, it is highly likely you will rediscover parts of yourself that have been repressed or buried under the clutter. These may include more laughter and lightness, increased creativity, richer emotional connections with yourself and with others, and more forgiveness and compassion.

All provide more reasons and opportunities for enjoyment. Of course enjoyment means different things to different people and we have many different ways of doing it to suit our individual tastes. However there are some general principles and pointers I want to share with you.

A meaningful life

With more space and time for reflection and consideration you will be better able to explore and live your true purpose: to live in a way that really matters to you and that you find fulfilling. A favourite quote of mine is by George Bernard Shaw:

This is the true joy in life, the being used for a purpose recognised by yourself as a mighty one, the being a force of nature instead of a feverish selfish little clod of ailments and grievances complaining that the world will not devote itself to making me happy.

I am of the opinion that my life belongs to the whole community and, as long as I live, it is my privilege to do for it whatever I can. I want to be thoroughly used up when I die, for the harder I work the more I live. I rejoice in life for its own sake. Life is no brief candle to me. It is a sort of splendid torch, which I've got to hold up for the moment and I want to make it burn as brightly as possible before handing it on to future generations.

This might sound exhausting and high energy but it isn't about that. It's about living with passion and focus and contributing fully.

Something else that will also make a big difference to the quality of your whole life is to:

Slow down

Slow down or even STOP. Most of us know how to take things at a run and sometimes that is required. It is often more challenging to actually slow down. In fact there is a whole movement spreading throughout the world encouraging us to do just that. From slow food to slow sex to slowing down with our children, it is all about living really consciously and totally enjoying and focusing on the moment. This also allows us to respond to life rather than simply reacting. (STOP is a useful acronym for Stop Think Options Proceed.) You don't have to live your life at 90 miles an hour to be effective – in fact doing so may have exactly the opposite effect.

Simplify

In her insightful and life-affirming book *The Top Five Regrets of the Dying* Bronnie Ware, a former palliative care nurse, describes what she has learnt from years of working with people at the end of their lives. She was amazed by the uniformity of the regrets people expressed to her. Every single male patient she nursed said, 'I wish I hadn't worked so hard'. She discussed with many of them how by simplifying your lifestyle and making conscious choices you don't necessarily need the money you think you do. Take the time to reassess your values and adjust your lifestyle while you can. Because it really matters. Don't postpone your happiness for anything.

Practise enjoying things without needing to own them. Visit museums and shrines, don't live in them. Leave stones on the beach where they belong. Reach out to others to borrow and lend: lawn mowers, cake tins, fancy dress, a cup of sugar – and enjoy the opportunities for interaction with other people that brings.

Choose your friends wisely

As you make adjustments to the way you live you may well find that some people disappear from your life because they just don't fit any more or you don't fit with them. It is all part of the ebb and flow. It is just another area where you can exercise more choice and awareness of how you spend your time and who you spend it with. I find it helpful to see people in two categories – as either 'radiators' or 'drains'. Those who seem to drain all the energy and spirit from you, and those who ignite it. Back in the 13th century the poet and Sufi mystic Rumi was advising people to 'Set your life on fire. Seek those who fan your flames,' and that advice holds good today.

The attitude of gratitude

Cultivating and practising the appreciation of everything in your life – exactly as it is – is a very enriching thing to do. All problems of attitude start when you believe you know how things should be, how other people should be, or how you tell yourself you should be. When you live with more acceptance of how things actually are you will experience more contentment. By exercising a degree of emotional detachment and compassionate curiosity, you will be able to see things more realistically and less emotionally and you can make decisions based on that reality.

You will see there are some things you can't change – other people for example, and some things you can – yourself and your attitudes and behaviours. Then you can focus your attention and energy on what and where you will really make a difference.

Learn to live with the imperfect, including yourself. Let go of striving for perfection – it is a goal that is impossible to obtain. Constantly striving for perfection will make you dissatisfied and miserable. Make things as good as you can: know you have given it your very best shot and that is enough.

And finally:

Don't forget to smell the roses.

Luxuriate in all the simple pleasures in life: start writing down what you notice and appreciate every day and what you are grateful for.

Remember that what you pay attention to will grow. So pay attention to the **ROSE** system – **R**ecognise, **O**rganise, **S**ystemise and **E**njoy! on a regular basis and watch your whole life bloom.

KEY LEARNING POINTS

- Keeping on top of your clutter is vital and it's a lot easier than sorting it in the first place.

- Make regular reviews a feature. If something isn't working, change it.

- Keep to your commitments and exercise self-discipline. New behaviour can be fun.

- 🐘 Take responsibility, avoid blaming others and aim for co-operation and harmony.

- 🐘 Making provision for your legacy is a key part to living a responsible life – make a will and keep it up to date.

- 🐘 Use the **ROSE** system as the four cornerstones of your life.

- 🐘 Say no to things you don't need or haven't got room for and activities you don't want to do.

- 🐘 Say yes to new ways of behaving and positive changes.

- 🐘 Enjoy a life that is meaningful for you with more space in your diary.

- 🐘 Slow down and simplify wherever you can. Don't postpone happiness.

- 🐘 Adopt the attitude of gratitude.

- 🐘 Don't forget to smell the roses.

BIBLIOGRAPHY AND RESOURCES

For your convenience, here is a list of the books I have mentioned directly or indirectly:

Allen, David, *Getting Things Done: The Art of Stress-Free Productivity*, Penguin, 2003.

Frankl, Viktor, E., *Man's Search for Meaning*, Rider, 2004. (Original German edition published in 1946.)

Honoré, Carl, *In Praise of Slow*, Orion, 2004.

Jeffers, Susan, *Feel the Fear and Do It Anyway*, Century 1987, 20th Anniversary edition 2007.

Ware, Bronnie, *The Top Five Regrets of the Dying*, Hay House, 2011.

Wienrich, Stephanie and Speyer, Josefine (eds) *The Natural Death Handbook*, Rider 2003.

This book comes under the category of self-help. If you think you require professional advice of a more therapeutic nature in the UK you could contact The British Association for Counselling and Psychotherapy (BACP) at www.bacp.co.uk or on 01455 883300.

If you ever find things get too much and you need somebody to talk to, the Samaritans are there 24 hours a day 365 days of the year. See www.samaritans.org for your local number or call 08457 90 90 90.

If you are interested in personal development courses run by the More to Life Foundation in many countries round the world, go to www.moretolife.org.

There are many and various alternative healing modalities available which help with the flow of energy through the body. The Emotion Code is one such. You can find out more at www.drbradleynelson.com.

NEXT STEPS

Congratulations if you have read this far. Many people don't read books to the end so you are clearly somebody with commitment. I hope this book has encouraged you to commit whole-heartedly to the process of clearing the clutter from your life and to creating rich new possibilities.

I've shared with you my **ROSE** system and other processes I use with my clients, but at the end of the day this is just a book. You might find you need more personal support, especially if you find the emotional issues to be particularly challenging.

You may be interested in attending a clutter-clearing workshop or in working with me privately.

In any event, please feel free to email me at victoria@eatthatelephant.co.uk or call me on 07773 503026, to discuss options. I will be delighted to hear from you.

Alternatively visit my website, www.eatthatelephant.co.uk where you can learn more about the coaching and support I offer.

I look forward to hearing from you and in the meantime wish you much space, organisation and harmony in your life. Enjoy!

ABOUT THE AUTHOR

Even when I was a very little girl I loved sorting and organising things and labelling them. Somewhat ironically throughout my life since, I have had a lot of personal experience of the debilitating and negative effects of disorganisation and clutter, particularly within my own family who didn't seem to see things the same way as me.

The most significant challenge of all was with my mother and stepfather. One large bedroom of their house was piled high from floor to ceiling with my stepfather's stuff. He worked a lot from home and his business papers covered the dining table and a lot of the floor. My mother was a very sociable person but this made it impossible for her to have visitors to their home and led to cross words and bad feeling.

My step-father died without making a will and without ever sorting this room. My mother made some progress on clearing it and, having learned something from experience, made a summary will but died shortly after herself. On all fronts a generous but very messy, complicated and onerous legacy was left.

This was one of many first hand experiences which helped to fuel my passion for helping others organise and sort out their possessions, their systems and their lives. My mission is to use my natural abilities and inclinations and all my experience to help prevent anybody else from having to go through similar difficulties.

A good while ago now I graduated from university and embarked on a career in project management, administration and training in the corporate world. Then along came motherhood and other major life challenges and gradually I evolved to focus on my passion and become an independent coach and declutter expert.

For over 20 years now I have been an expert facilitator, coach and mentor. I am grateful to one of my own mentors, Daniel Wagner, for reminding me that 'obsessed is a word the lazy use to describe the dedicated'. I am absolutely dedicated to helping people clear and transform both their inner and outer landscapes.

One of my favourite quotes is from Isaac Newton. 'If I have seen further it is by standing on the shoulders of giants'. I am committed to continual personal and professional development and have studied with, among others, Brad Brown, Chris Howard, Karen Kingston, Katherine Woodward-Thomas and Tony Robbins.

Having said all that, I do see my greatest achievement as having raised two happy and fulfilled grown up sons. Mind you, being named one of the top 1 per cent most endorsed people in the UK for Personal Development on LinkedIn in 2012 was a proud moment too.

www.ingramcontent.com/pod-product-compliance
Lightning Source LLC
Chambersburg PA
CBHW030259100526
44590CB00012B/453